provo

provo

amsterdam's anarchist revolt

richard kempton

autonomedia

In memory of Suzanne Kempton-Gerson
The Hague 1940–Berkeley 2000
whose interest in the Provos inspired this book.

uxori carissimae

Book design: Josh MacPhee

Published by Autonomedia, PO Box 568, Williamsburgh Station,
Brooklyn, NY 11211-0568, USA.

Autonomedia publishes and distributes a wide variety of materials
on radical politics and culture. Please visit www.autonomedia.org
for a full catalog and more information.

State of the Arts
NYSCA

This publication is made possible in part with public funds from the New York State Council on the Arts, a state agency.

Printed in Canada

contents

acknowledgements

My interest in the Provo movement was initially kindled by a paper on the Provo use of the Dutch language written for a class at the University of California, Berkeley by my late wife, Suzanne Gerson, a native of the Netherlands. The impetus to write this book stemmed from conversations I had with Johan Snapper, Professor of Dutch at UC Berkeley.

Thanks are due to a number of people who aided me with their help, encouragement, and sometimes by supplying with needed publications from the Netherlands. Jaap van Ginneken, Sjoerd Wartena, and Tjebbe van Tijen, the successive directors of the Provo archives when it was at the University of Amsterdam, gave generously of their time and greatly aided my use of the archives; as did Peter De Jonge at a more recent date at the Internationaale Instituut voor Sociale Geschiedenis (International Institute for Social History), Amsterdam, which is the present location of the Provo archives.

The Dutch writer Simon Vinkenoog and Provo co-founder Roel van Duyn were kind enough to read early versions of the manuscript, provided copious commentary, and supplied publications otherwise not available to me. Provos Luud Schimmelpennink of Amsterdam and Herman J. Claeys of Brussels also gave generously of their time in speaking with me.

Dutch friends were helpful in answering numerous questions about details of Dutch political and social life and supplying me with publications and newspaper clippings. A very special word of appreciation is due to my brother-in-law Hans Gerson who has supplied me with much help and information over the years. Thanks are also due to the Oxenaar family of Arnhem and to Willem Malten, formerly of Amsterdam.

I owe a special debt of gratitude to Professor Gerald Larson, formerly of the University of California, Santa Barbara, who called my attention to Jean-Paul Sartre's neglected masterpiece, *The Critique of Dialectical Reason*, which I utilized in evaluating the revolutionary phenomenon of the 1960s. Thanks too to L. J., formerly of Amsterdam, who translated phrases of her native Amsterdam slang and architectural terms I could not find in dictionaries available to me. And thanks to others who either read my manuscript or encouraged me to pursue publication, among them William Timberman, John Rowe, Maurice Zeitlin, Richard Flacks, Joseph Adler, Daniel Marlin, Steve Williamson, Glenn and Colette Gauthier Myles, and Henk van Os.

I have learned much from Jordan Zinovich and my other editors at Autonomedia about the history of anarchism and its developments since the '60s and have hopefully incorporated these valuable lessons in the text of the book. And I benefited from the comments of Hans Plomp and Stephen Snelders, who read the edited manuscript on Autonomedia's behalf. Again, a word of heartfelt thanks is due. Also, thanks to Peter Stansill and David Zane Mairowitz for permission to use materials from their collection *BAMN (By Any Means Necessary): Outlaw Manifestos and Ephemera, 1965–70.*

I must add that the opinions and conclusions expressed are my own. In no way do they constitute an endorsement of my views on the part of those mentioned above — I am thinking here particularly of my Dutch contacts. It seems to be a point of Batavian pride that no two Dutch people will agree on any matter social or political, so I gracefully accept beforehand the possibility that no one in the Netherlands will be completely in accord with that which I have written about three years of their nation's history.

—Richard Kempton

publisher's foreword

Provo: Amsterdam's Anarchist Revolt is another title in Autonomedia's ongoing exploration of Dutch resistance movements: previously, *The Devil's Anarchy* (2005) examined early Dutch piracy, and *Cracking the Movement* (1994) chronicled the Dutch squatting movement.

While some in our collective cannot imagine modern anarchism without Provo, others only came to understand the movement's impact through researching and editing this book. Provo is a legendary movement whose creative energy, successes, and failures helped shape the anarchism that we practice and love today. And while the effects of legends often drift in and out of our everyday lives, they frequently pass unanalyzed. This book brings the history of Provo to the fore so that we can make the connections between the past and present, as well as take note of substantial differences between their historical moment and ours. Our hope for this introductory history of Provo in English audience is that it allows others to mine Provo's experiments and experiences for inspiration and strategies.

Provo's playful combination of theory and street-level practice helped generate the creative and flexible engagement that has become an essential part of our most effective interventions into the increasingly militarized and regulated spaces of our everyday lives. It is part of a hidden history of fleeting moments, outbursts, and insurgencies that connect to form a linked revolutionary history, one which often remains secret even to those who make it. Many people involved in Provo likely were not aware of the ways in which previous revolutionary traditions informed them, and likewise, Provo has "invisibly" informed current practices of creative resistance. This book hopes to uncover parts of the hidden history that we're already embodying and living through even if we're not totally aware of it.

Provo initiated the programs of playful street insurrection that we picked up and expanded through events such as Critical Mass and Reclaim the Streets. The White Housing Plan was an important precursor for the squatting movement that emerged in Amsterdam and elsewhere in Europe, eventually spreading to North America. Furthermore, the White Bicycles intervention, which Amsterdam authorities had seen as such a threat, is now copied around the world and are often sponsored and funded by municipal authorities.

But such tactics are only the beginning of what we can learn from Provo. The Provos found ways to expand temporary autonomous zones into a sustainable movement that were based on collective processes, critical reflection, and an impulse towards action. Rather than isolating the spheres of contemplation, politics, protest, and play, they valued informed theories that generated new practices through critical reflection. There is much to learn from the particular ways they worked these levels simultaneously.

Even the death of Provo was a strategic move stemming from a consensus-based process of self-reflection. It was initiated by the movement itself: when the Provos realized that their cohesion was waning, they determined that dispersal was more strategic than continuation. Their conscious choice of public dissolution demonstrated Provo's true vitality. That choice enabled them to join and inspire other groups, and we need only scrutinize the foundations of the practices of resistance in Amsterdam today to recognize the continuing impact they have.

Provo does not stand alone. It lies embedded in a matrix of earlier movements, as well as countless later layerings. There is clear evidence that the 1968 Paris activists borrowed from Provo's successes. So even the Situationists — who are often canonized within various radical milieus — owe a debt to the creative Provo activists who played with the political potential of aesthetics.

It is sometimes surprising to realize that our histories are so incomplete, and a project like this by no means completes the history of Provo. In the DIY spirit, we take this opportunity to encourage others to pick up this thread and explore it on their own. For instance, any future work must include a feminist analysis — on our part we have not even managed to provide a translation of the anti-patriarchy initiatives outlined in the White Wives Plan. Deeper studies of the relationships between Provo and the other political and anti-war movements in Amsterdam would also add a great deal to our understanding of the movement. A closer examination of how Provo organized itself, and whether the social initiatives they developed emerged from innovative ways of working together, would also be a welcome avenue of research.

Nevertheless, we hope that this small compilation that includes narrative texts, appended speculations and documents, illustrations, a map, and an extensive annotated bibliography will encourage further analysis of Provo's strengths and weaknesses.

In the spirit of Provo this project was collectively produced, with sustained input from Lindsay Caplan, Josh McPhee, Ben Meyers, Erika Biddle, Hans Plomp, Stephen Snelders, Spencer Sunshine, Stevphen Shukaitis, and Jordan Zinovich. Richard Kempton sent us an uncut gem. We're proud of the flawed jewel our combined efforts produced. May this contribution to our secret history from below prove viral, infecting others with the urge to follow Provo's lead.

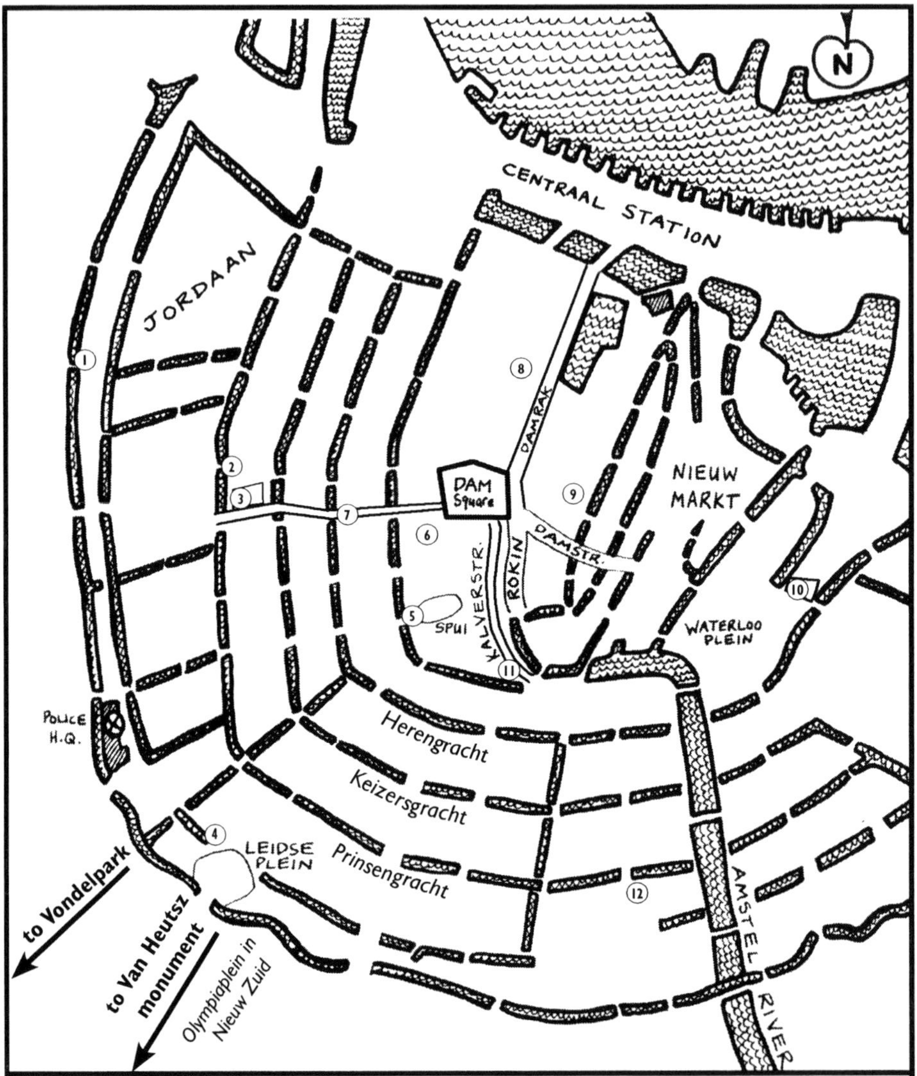

KEY TO PROVO AMSTERDAM

1. **Site of Jan Weggelaar's death** *Marnixstraat, near the Marnixplantsoen*
2. **Anne Frank House** *Prinsengracht, next to the Westerkerk*
3. **Westerkerk** *Prinsengracht at the Rozengracht*
4. **Anti-Smoking Temple** *Korte Leidsedwaarsstraat, near the Leidsegracht*
5. **Lieverdje** *Het Spui, at the Singel*
6. **De Telegraaf offices** *Nieuwezijds Voorburgwal, south of the Paleisstraat*
7. **Raadhuisstraat** *West from the back of the Dam Palace*
8. **Site of Floris Schaper shooting** *Oudebrugsteeg, off the Damrak, across from the north end of the Beurs van Berlage.*
9. **Oude Raadhuis (Stadhuis)** *Oudezijds Voorburgwal, south of the Damstraat*
10. **Dokwerker monument** *Jonas Daniel Meyerplein*
11. **Kalverstraat**
12. **Polak & Van Gennep Gallery** *Prinsengracht near the Reguliersgracht*

introduction

In the mid-1960s, the political and artistic imagination of the Netherlands was seized by a unique and bizarre political movement known as Provo. Sparked by a fatally-timed pun, Provo sprang into birth full-grown, almost overnight, and succeeded in fomenting a year-long rebellion in the heart of the Dutch capital that culminated explosively in a spontaneous five-day riot on June 14th, 1966. Provo made a lasting impression in the Netherlands, changing the course of Dutch political life and helping transform Amsterdam into a legendary Mecca for an emerging international counter-culture. Though the Provo movement is not well known outside of Belgium and the Netherlands, it was one of the most stunning of the cultural revolutions of the '60s. Bits and pieces of the Provo legend have been woven, here and there, into the mythology of the period. Non-Dutch readers, however, have never had the opportunity to become better acquainted with the movement because little about it has been published that isn't in Dutch. This small contribution is a first step towards breaking that silence.

After 1966 the Netherlands was forever changed. One obvious transformation has been the de-facto, if not de-jure, acceptance of the use of soft drugs such as marijuana, hashish, LSD, psilocybin, and mescaline, making the Netherlands a pioneer in unofficially but openly tolerating the "soft" drug subculture. One effect that Provo and related movements of the time had was to push a smug middle-class social democracy far enough to the left that on two separate occasions the Dutch parliament publicly disassociated itself from the efforts of the United States in Vietnam. Provo's strategies and tactics assisted in activating a solid political base for a renewed Left and initiated a resurgent Anarchism in the Netherlands: eventually helping inspire the student seizure of the *Maagdehuis* (the administrative building of the University of Amsterdam) in 1969 and the creation of the Kabouter movement in 1970 — movements that promised to take even wider hold on Dutch political life before they too faded out. In fact, a host of imaginative new movements hatched from the Provo incubator, including the ecological *Paniek-Zaaiers* (Panic Planters), the squatters, and the many activist neighborhood groups even now willing to keep Amsterdam's political pot boiling and its imagination stirred. And after Provo enthusiastically promoted it, the Netherlands, which before then had been the most puritanical of countries, became an acknowledged center of the sexual revolution.

Though Scandinavia was at that time more widely known for its militant social democracies and its active promotion of the sexual revolution — both of which were opposed in the Netherlands by politically organized, strongly entrenched religious and puritanical traditions — the Scandinavian countries couldn't match Provo's unique blend of anarchism and avant-garde performance art. A Provo-led resistance that began as a humble one-man anti-tobacco campaign in 1962 swelled to climax in the five-day Battle of Amsterdam in June 1966.

I decided to write this book in the 1970s only when I realized that no one else intended to write an English-language account of the Provos. The editors and I have worked hard to expand and complete that original manuscript. Most of the original publications on Provo were in Dutch, but *Delta* magazine, a semi-official English-language quarterly of Dutch culture published in Amsterdam, brought out one special *Provo* issue (Volume 10, #3, Autumn 1967). *Delta*'s coverage is surprisingly pro-Provo and copies of the issue are available in many libraries. However, *Delta* concentrated on the 1966 political phase of the movement and avoided looking at the rich artistic and drug scenes to which it was connected. The half-dozen book-length treatments published in Dutch and listed in the bibliography of this book were my main sources of information. By drawing from them I have tried to provide a narration of the Provo movement up to the moment it peaked, and I have included a series of appendices that help translate and interpret it within the context of the social milieu of the country.

I've made an effort to concentrate on the early "Happening" phase of the movement, which in my view has been understudied — particularly the career of Robert Jasper Grootveld as a "Happener-magician" (1962–65). It is perhaps natural that the purest and most inspired creative acts of humanity should exist only as partially recorded deeds, unheralded in history save for the long shadow they cast on events that follow them. I wish to emphasize the artistic aspects of Provo: its conscious use of the Happening, which was extraordinarily "avant-garde"; its imaginative use of language; the relationship of many Provo concepts to the developing drug subculture. These aspects of the movement are too often avoided by avowedly "political" writers. Further, I try to show how the Provos effectively used art forms in the service of social revolution, converting social and political life into a provocative theatrical confrontation between activist and authority, protestor and police. This tactical stance, borrowed in part from a concept in a Dutch academic dissertation on juvenile delinquency, gave Provo its name and its modus operandi.

The purely political aspects of the movement are certainly important. But much of what has been published in Dutch is dogmatically biased, particularly in its attempt to be rational. The success of Provo was largely a success of imaginative empirical political action dictated by the general mood of the moment. My narrative follows events as they unfolded, without trying to evaluate them too theoretically. Indeed, by 1966 everything was moving so quickly that it would have been very difficult for the Provos to act within a consistent theoretical framework. It is beside the point to criticize them for this "failure"; their revolutionary Time created its own impetus.

Briefly stated, Provo was the marriage of two youthful social elements: the "hip" audience that attended Robert Jasper Grootveld's magic Happenings every Saturday at midnight, and the leftist remnants of the Ban-the-Bomb movement (the Dutch Aldermaston marchers in Great Britain). Both elements turned anarchist in 1965, at the ripe moment when the Dutch crown princess, Beatrix, decided upon a politically controversial marriage. The Dutch monarchy, the war in Vietnam, and air pollution from automobiles became Provo's major issues, and the movement's development played out against the complex background of the peculiarly Dutch "*Zuilen* system" (pronounced "Zow" [as in "south"]-"len," meaning pillars).

The pillars of the Zuilen system were both secular and religious groupings: the Catholics, Protestants, social-democrats, and non-religious "liberals" (i.e., business interests) amounted to a tight clustering of clearly defined vertical interest groups with multiple connections to labor and capital. Political influence in the country was diluted and divided four ways, which tended to frustrate every genuine attempt at political or social change. (A particularly informative book on the subject is Arend Lijphart's monograph, *The Politics of Accommodation: Pluralism and Democracy in the Netherlands.*)

Historically, Holland was once a medieval province of Burgundy, then of the Spanish Hapsburg empire, and finally of the Dutch Republic (the United Provinces of the Netherlands) that now comprises two modern provinces, North Holland (Amsterdam, Haarlem) and South Holland (The Hague, Rotterdam, Delft, Leiden)

— two of the eleven provinces of the country we know as the Netherlands (the Lowlands). Holland accounts for 16% of the land area of the Netherlands and is home to 67% of the population. (Referring to the Netherlands as Holland is comparable to referring to the United Kingdom as England, though during national festivals the Dutch often happily call themselves "Hollanders.")

The national language is *Nederlands*, which used to be known as *Hollands*. It is closely related to German and English, sitting somewhere midway between those two languages. In English, *Nederlands* is known as *Dutch*, taking its name from *Diets* (pronounced "Deets") its medieval forerunner. Seventeen million people in the Netherlands and six million in Belgium — the Flemish — speak Dutch. (The differences between Flemish and Dutch are comparable to the difference between the English spoken in London and New York.) Provo caught on quickly in Belgium and was somewhat influential in Germany, Switzerland, Italy, the United Kingdom and the United States, but cut off as it was by the too-effective barrier of the Dutch language, it never really blossomed as an international movement. This linguistic barrier has largely marginalized modern Dutch literary and intellectual accomplishments: I refer here to both the postwar literary renaissance of the 1950s and Provo. In my view it would be a pity for a movement as fascinating as Provo to remain in the shadows. I hope that this short history can serve both to introduce the subject and to foster new interest in and further research on the history of the anarchist movements of the '60s and '70s.

works referenced

Delta: A Review of Arts, Life and Thought in the Netherlands (1967); Lijphart (1975).

1. amsterdam, the magic center (1961–1965)

The Provo movement was born in a city that has taken part in many of the avant-garde movements of the past 100 years. Amsterdam is one of the magnetic European centers that, like Paris, Copenhagen, Munich, Berlin, Rome and Vienna, boasts rich cultural traditions and a witty, intelligent population sympathetic to inventive forms of human expression. In certain ways it is similar to the San Francisco that nurtured the Beat, Digger, and Hippie movements half a century ago.

Since the late 19th century, innovative art and literary movements have developed throughout the Netherlands. The Haagse School (a circle of painters in The Hague) influenced the early work of Vincent Van Gogh. *Nieuwe Kunst* (the Dutch Art Nouveau movement), the Amsterdam School of architecture, and Dutch Dadaists like Theo Van Doesburg all impacted the wider European scenes of their day. *De Stijl* movement (pronounced like "style" in English) was the Dutch equivalent of the Bauhaus and included such radical innovators as Piet Mondriaan, Van Doesburg, and the architect Gerrit Rietveld. And it was an active Dutch Surrealist, the novelist and journalist Harry Mulisch, who penned the first book on the Provo movement *Bericht Aan De Rattenkoning (Report to the King of the Rats)*; the title is an unflattering reference to authoritarian bureaucrats.

It is not generally known that the Netherlands remained neutral during World War I, but that fact had important repercussions. After 1918, the dominant Calvinist ideologues took self-satisfied credit for the country's good fortune in escaping the ravages that had fallen on its less fortunate neighbors like Catholic Belgium. In 1939 and 1940, as advancing German armies fanned across Europe, the Netherlands expected to remain neutral once again. So the shock of the German invasion in World War II dislocated the smug and stifling middle class that had ruled for much of the previous 300 years. The German invasion and the loss of the Dutch colonial empire in Indonesia crippled both the elite's self-image and the country's economy. These events created a gulf between the pre-war and post-war generations in the country, and post-war economic affluence gave many people a level of material abundance that they had never known before. The post-war generation grew up dissatisfied with workaday life and found the values of their parents and their nation unfulfilling and cramped. Gradually, the stage was set for the youthful rebellion that came in the 1960s.

It was amidst the atmosphere of historical shock that vital new art forms developed shortly after 1945. In 1947, the COBRA movement brought the trend of abstract painting to Amsterdam. COBRA is an acronym made up of the initial letters of the three cities central to the movement: COpenhagen, BRussels and Amsterdam. The leading Dutch figures in the movement were Karel Appel, Corneille, Constant Nieuwenhuys, and Lucebert. COBRA tied itself closely to an emerging group of Dutch poets, *De Vijftigers* (pronounced "Five-Tiggers" and meaning Writers of the Fifties), as well as to the Lettrists and Situationists in France. Lucebert, for instance, was eminent both as a COBRA painter and a Vijftiger poet. And Constant Nieuwenhuys was instrumental in shaping the Situationist urban aesthetic. Initially, the Netherlands' Calvinist cultural critics laughed away the new artists, but by 1954, after a seven-year struggle, free verse and abstractionism were dominant modes in Dutch artistic life.

The Vijftigers attained their crowning moment in what is best described as a Happening, though it would be five years before that term attained international cultural currency. In 1954, Lucebert was awarded the municipal prize for poetry by the city of Amsterdam. He arrived at the presentation ceremony at the Stedelijk Museum, the city's modern art museum, as the "Emperor of the Vijftigers," crowned and triumphantly sporting velvet and ermine robes. He was accompanied by a queen and several armed attendants (including other Vijftiger poets). When confused museum officials telephoned the Burgemeester, Amsterdam's mayor, the police appeared and forcibly escorted the Emperor-Poet and his entourage from the building. Provoking a police response to art would become an important recurring tactic for the next 15 years, and Lucebert's coronation burns like a flame in the historical memory of the period as the flaring climax of one movement heralding a flickering on the horizon. It was a magnificent symbolic gesture; a "symptom," as Robert Jasper Grootveld, the prophet of Provo, might have phrased it.

During the years following Lucebert's triumph, Dutch literature flourished. Writers grew considerably in their ability, displaying a supple mastery equal to the best writing appearing elsewhere in Europe and the Americas. As the short story and novel became favored forms, some of the Vijftigers transformed themselves into major novelists. The most celebrated writers were Willem Frederik Hermans and Gerard Kornelis Van Het Reve (later writing under the *nom de guerre* Gerard Reve). Neither Hermans nor Reve were Viftigers, but the ex-Vijftigers Remco Campert and Hugo Claus (a Belgian who published in the Netherlands) also produced important work, and a new school of poets, the Zestigers (Poets of the Sixties), experimented with concrete and sound poetry. Included in the Zestigers group was Johnny the Selfkicker (Johan Van Doorn), who would figure prominently in the Amsterdam Happenings scene. Simon Vinkenoog, another Viftiger, became the spiritual voice of the psychedelic subculture of 1960s Amsterdam.

The new writing hit hard at the core of the Dutch self-image of that period, for it was critical in both its form and content. In his novel *The Darkroom of Damocles*, published in an English translation by Macmillan in London in 1965, Willem Frederik Hermans questioned the vaunted wartime heroism of his countrymen. Gerard Reve's novel *De Avonden (The Evenings)* proclaimed that postwar Dutch cultural life lacked all significant content. The impact of such books on the Netherlands was profound, and some of the writers, including Hermans, Reve, and, in Belgium, Claus, were brought to trial on charges of offending public morality.

happenings

Throughout the 1960s, Amsterdam was receptive to the new art forms coursing through Western Europe. Dutch poetry and painting grew ever more abstract, and Dutch composers embraced electronic music. From 1964 to 1968, the city became the European base for the Living Theater of Julian Beck and Judith Malina. It should come as no surprise, then, that Amsterdam was early in welcoming that dynamic formal catalyst for change and transformation, the Happening.

The performance that gave this art form its name was "Eighteen Happenings in Six Parts," staged in New York by Allen Kaprow in 1959. In 1947, Kaprow had initiated his career by enrolling in Hans Hofmann's painting school. Under Hofmann's tutelage he developed a style of action painting and, along with a number of his classmates, he co-founded a cooperative artists' gallery on East 10th Street in Greenwich Village named the Hansa Gallery (a homage to Hofmann). By 1952, Kaprow was exhibiting his first "assemblages," or mounted constructions.

The art movement known as Abstract Expressionism had developed simultaneously in Europe and New York, springing from

Dada and Surrealism. Although New York critics had baptized them "Abstract Expressionists," the painters themselves preferred to use terms like "Concrete Painting" or "Action Painting" to describe what they were doing. In New York the style was best exemplified by the work of Jackson Pollock and Willem de Kooning, an American painter born in the Netherlands. Influenced by Pollock and by Abstract Expressionism's devotion to process and action, Kaprow developed what he called an "action-collage" technique wherein his assemblages incorporated various innovative materials, including straw, twine, and flashing lights.

Between 1956 and 1958, Kaprow studied musical composition under the direction of John Cage at the New School for Social Research in Manhattan. Cage's notions of chance and indeterminacy as aesthetic values became fundamental to both Kaprow's theorizing and to his artistic activity. All experimentation was valid to Cage, whose own impulse at the time was towards theater — where he believed the most effective integration of art and "reality" could be found. As Kaprow's action-collages grew in size, incorporating aspects of sound and performance, they reached the point where they filled entire art galleries and situated the spectators in all-encompassing "environments." The final evolution of the "Happening" took place when Kaprow began "scoring" activities for the audience members, whom he viewed as integral parts of his environments.

Other artists in New York took up the new art form. Groups of various sizes, barely distinguishing performers from spectators, incorporated spontaneous movement and inexplicable or everyday activities in their Happenings. Activities as mundane as sweeping the floor appeared absurd when incorporated into Happenings because they either lacked context or contrasted with other activities. Happenings and their audiences were juxtaposed or were disconnected from settings like Grand Central Station in New York. One early Happening featured two grand pianos on stage alongside two walls, each of which had a small hole in it. Two teams competed to get their piano first through the hole in their partition. One's own reaction to my description of the "piano Happening" should serve as an adequate definition of Happenings in general. Stories of Happenings and their absurd activities spread widely by word of mouth, and the reactions to such descriptions expanded the influence and importance of each event.

Though there is some film footage of Happenings, the personal emotional impact of the actual events is lacking and can only be grasped intellectually. Most of the original American Happenings occurred in New York before 1964, and few have been performed since then. However, Germany became the European point of departure for the form, which arrived in the Netherlands around 1962. Michael Kirby, an authority on the subject, writes that Happenings were hard to find, were rarely performed, and that the number of people who actually saw them was small. We must therefore depend on secondary sources for information about them, which is somewhat like trying to understand a painting without having seen one.

Kirby compares Happenings to a three-ring circus, an art form without "information structure" but with simultaneous compartmentalization. While they were carefully planned, the programmed activities seemed to lack content because they were structure, and only structure. The content was supplied by the audience in its reaction to and interpretation of the experience. Kirby calls Happenings "non-matrixed," which is to say that the performer is not integrated into the activity he is performing but is simply himself and expressing his own emotions. For example, a performer sweeping the floor is not Hamlet with a broom but simply engaged in certain prescribed actions. Altering the understanding of performers in this way alters the role of the audience as well. Audiences moved around, shouted, and performed as choruses according to instructions handed out as they entered a theatrical space. Each Happening depended on the audience to complete it by means of its own performance and understanding of what was going on, regardless of the careful planning that the organizers had put into the event. A Happening was always a catalyst. Curious juxtapositions of everyday objects and activities in ridiculous situations and incongruous locations served to corrode our culture's arbitrary sense of reality and the intolerable boundary between art and life. This strategy serves to destroy the traditionally passive role of the audience, creating what amounts to a revolutionary new situation, given the right circumstances.

happenings in amsterdam

The earliest Happening in Amsterdam was *Open Het Graf (Open the Grave)*, which was organized on December 9, 1962 by Simon Vinkenoog and two Americans, Melvin Clay and Frank Stern. *Open Het Graf* was staged specifically to introduce the notion of the Happening to the Dutch public. It honored the dead. Though the title was a satire of a 24-hour Dutch television marathon for flood relief, *Open Het Dorp (Open the Village)*, it is remarkably similar to Kaprow's *A Service for the Dead*, which was performed earlier that same year. This connection suggests a direct link between the New York and Amsterdam scenes.

While New York Happenings tended to be highly structured, sometimes even requiring rehearsals, the Dutch Happenings

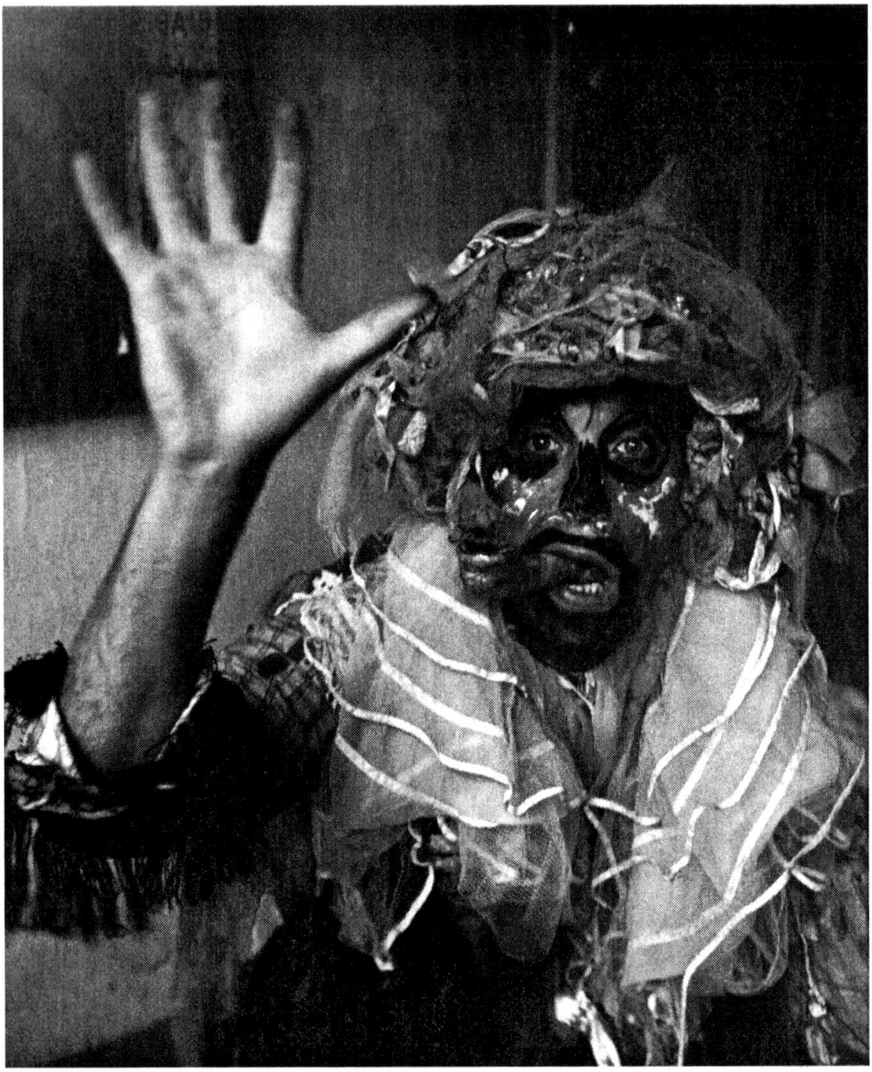

Robert Jasper Grootveld in full Happening warpaint.

evoked a more spontaneous note, being what Kirby called "improvised events" executed by gifted and inspired eccentrics. They were far wackier than the New York Happenings, which were quite intellectual in concept. Among the more interesting of the early Happenings in Amsterdam was an Ice-Happening in the home of Fred Wessels, a painter who was later associated with Robert Jasper Grootveld's pre-Provo anti-nicotine campaign. Wessels lived in the bohemian Jordaan district. During one spell of freezing weather, he turned on all the faucets in his home and propped the windows open, allowing an ice rink to form. A woman then skated the rink in a pair of *klompen*, Dutch wooden shoes.

Poet and performer Johnny the Self-Kicker soon began writing scenarios for Happenings. He called himself a "free-jazz speaker of the anti-jazz," describing his work as anti-theater and stating that the age of the individual artist was finished. Gerrit the Ether Sniffer, who eventually had to give up his chosen means of tripping because it threatened his life, accompanied the Self-Kicker's Happenings on the saxophone.

Stoned in the Streets, a famous Dutch Happening of 1964, was more a series of outlandish nightclub acts than the Happening it purported to be. Dr. Bart Huges, a medical intern and advocate of psychedelic drugs, had bored a hole in his forehead, a "Third Eye," that gave him a permanent high. His successful operation was unveiled at the Happening when the bandages on his head were unwound to the accompaniment of a drum salvo. Johnny the Self-Kicker got himself high in his usual fashion, by chanting at a shout, and then danced through the audience with the bust of a department store mannequin. Marijke Koger, the self-styled "Hippest Chick in Town," did a slow striptease of seven thin dresses that finally revealed her nude body completely covered in paint.

Although these Dutch Happenings were inane to a point that taxed the form, they retained the defining components of the New York Happenings: they demanded audience participation and required meticulous structuring (or planning), and they fulfilled themselves in an audience's reaction to what it was experiencing. The Happening was a totally open form with unlimited possibilities for exploitation, and it was in Amsterdam, the passionately adored "Magic Center" of the Dutch avant-garde, that it would be put to stunning new uses by a gifted new master.

works referenced

Haftmann (1960); Huges (1966/1967); Kaprow (no date); Kirby (1966); Meier (1966); Mulisch (1967).

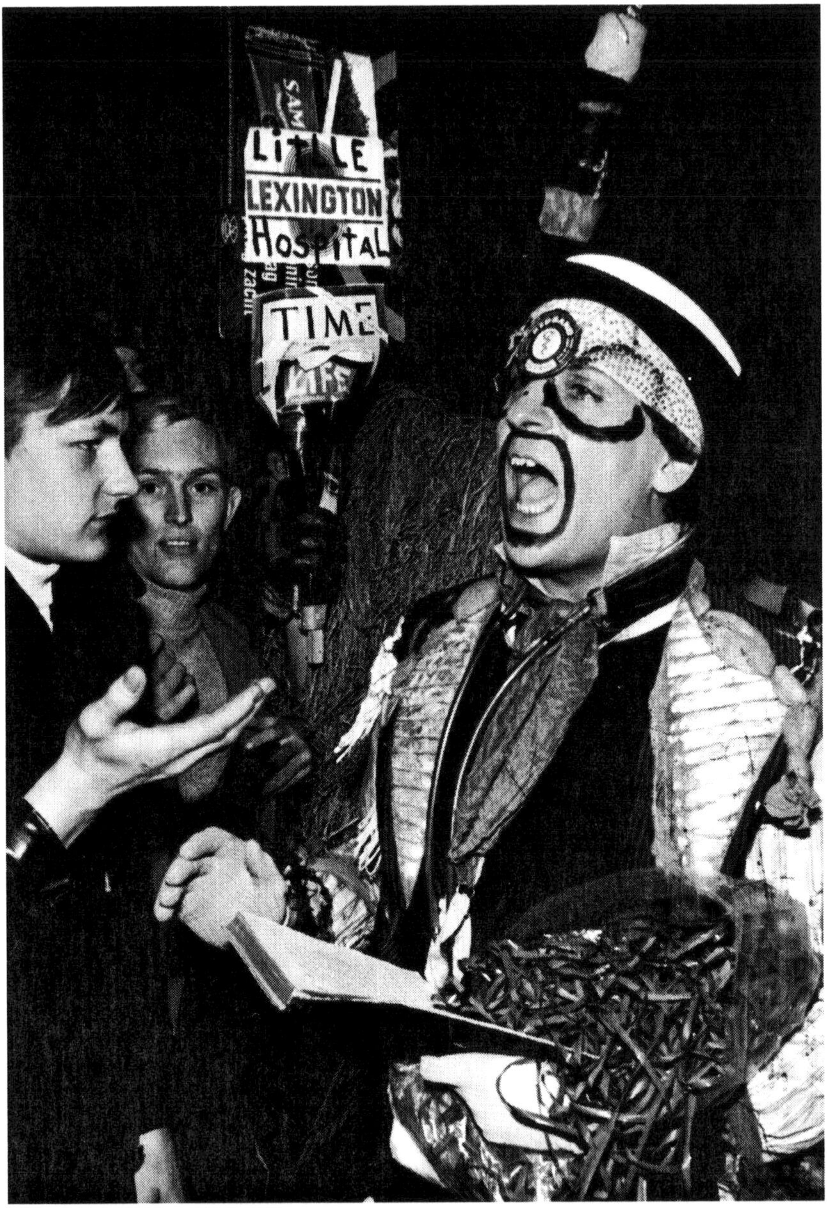

Happening performance by Robert Jasper Grootveld at the Lieverdje.

2. the prophet of magic amsterdam: robert jasper grootveld

Robert Jasper Grootveld, the Prophet of Amsterdam, was a genius of the absurd. He relished carrying his strong convictions against tobacco and nicotine addiction to creative and extreme conclusions. Though his performative rationale hung together intellectually, the actual expression of his ideas bordered on sublime inanity, often illuminated by an uncanny penchant for accurate prophetic prediction. Much of what was going on in Amsterdam by 1965 seemed due to the fact that Robert Jasper Grootveld had willed it. And by then he had been busy for four years with the bizarre incantations that came to serve as trademarks of Amsterdam's '60s heritage.

Grootveld himself never wrote much, save for some manifestos and one short article. However, two Dutch journalists, Dick P. J. Van Reeuwijk and Henk Meier, have published books about Amsterdam's hectic alternative lifestyles in the early '60s and have managed to capture much of Grootveld's flair. The earliest accounts of the Provo movement, written by politically oriented observers who didn't care to delve into the drug culture or the complex artistic phenomenon of the Happenings, either ignore Grootveld or gloss over his activities with a few general statements. However, the prophet should be restored to his rightful position and his genius accorded the recognition it deserves if Provo is to be fully appreciated in its miraculous and artistic dimensions.

Robert Jasper Grootveld was born on July 19, 1932 in Amsterdam. His father was an anarchist, a recognized member of a community with a rich tradition in the history of the city. Grootveld himself was a school dropout who got much of his education through working some sixty-odd jobs, becoming a furniture maker, an advertising copywriter, a window dresser, a window washer, a seaman, and a hospital janitor, among other occupations, before assuming the role of full-time happener.

Grootveld's diverse work history shaped many of his ideals

and future interventions. He worked for one five-year stretch as a window washer at the Hirsch Building on the Leidseplein, a public square ringed with cafés in the center of Amsterdam. During that time he spent a week living on a life raft afloat in the Amsterdam canals, cooking over a camp stove and wearing a different suit every day. The unusual stunt captured the interest of the local newspapers, which picked up his story. He says that that was when he learned the power of publicity. He also bought a *bakfiets* (pronounced Bock-Feets), a kind of bicycle-powered pick-up truck, on the sides of which he painted "Amsterdam-Paris." Friends urged him to peddle the contraption to Paris, following the logic of the message it bore. Thinking to join the Paris cabaret scene as a transvestite performer, he took them up on their advice and spent months pedaling south before returning to Amsterdam.

Seeking change, and open to every opportunity afforded him, Grootveld subsequently sailed to Africa as a seaman aboard a Dutch ship. Once there he was struck by the resemblance between tribal ritual and what he called the addiction of the consumer in modern society, particularly by what he termed the idolatry of cigarette smokers. On his return, he likened smokers to sacrificial victims, condemned to the terrible fate of lung cancer. Increasingly he remarked on the fact that the concrete pillars around Amsterdam used for commercial advertising were often papered with cigarette ads. Grootveld referred to them as the totem poles of the Western Asphalt Jungle, and noted that the most prominent Dutch tobacco company was called *Kerkhof*, a family name that means "cemetery" in Dutch. He decided that the time had come to protest. Resenting his own life-threatening addiction to nicotine, he resolved to become a one-man anti-smoking movement — a "charlatan, a simple and inadequate exhibitionist" — whose goal would be to outlaw cigarette advertising in the Netherlands.

With nicotine as his focus, Grootveld considered himself a fanatical social worker more concerned with the problem of addiction in the modern world than driven by a thirst for revenge against the tobacco industry. In part, his own addiction prompted him to choose tobacco as the target of his protests, but it was a widespread reliance on all drugs, including tobacco, and the Dutch addiction to television and consumerism that he hoped to discourage. He derided the obsessive need to buy motorcycles, television sets, and electric eggbeaters, which bear the delightful name of *roomkloppers* (pronounced Roam-Kloppers). He hoped that a solution to the problems of addiction and consumerism would arise dialectically when he confronted them with an opposing point of view.

Grootveld recalled his father telling him about the five evil Ks: *Kerk*, *Kapitaal*, *Kroeg*, *Krommenie*, and *Kazerne* (Church, Capital,

Bars, Krommenie — a factory town notorious for its use of child labor in the 19th century — and Barracks, meaning the Army). He noted the introduction of tobacco from colonial America, but believed that the Indians may have smoked something more psychedelic in their peace pipes. It was his opinion that the cigarette had replaced the Cross in modern life. He compared the habit of smoking in contemporary society to the human sacrifices of the Incas. Intending to offset the sacrificial ritual of smoking with the alternative rituals that Happenings could provide, he embarked on a course that brought him increasingly into the public's view.

Grootveld's first direct action was to chalk up the cigarette ads with the word "*Kanker*" (cancer) or simply the letter "K." Several of his friends joined in the cause, and it was only a matter of time before K became synonymous with cancer in Amsterdam. This hurt the advertising firms, which brought a successful lawsuit against him. Because he had no money to pay his fine he was sentenced to sixty days in jail. Shortly after his release he was returned to jail for another sixty days because the Ks began reappearing. Only widespread publicity of his message could combat the expensive advertising the tobacco companies employed. The K campaign, combined with his flair for exhibitionism, earned Grootveld the press coverage and publicity he needed to take his next step.

After his successive jail terms, Grootveld moved his anti-smoking campaign to an abandoned shed near the Leidseplein. The shed was owned by Nicolaas Kroese, sympathetic owner of the *Vijf Vliegen* (Five Flies), a renowned Amsterdam restaurant. Grootveld called it the "Anti-Smoking Temple," and inside it he led his collaborators, primarily artists and local teenagers, in ritual performances against smoking and tobacco. Vast quantities of smoke were produced to exorcise evil spirits, with Grootveld leaping around the fires in ceremonial dress, his face painted and his spellbound audience circling the flames behind him. His tongue-in-cheek sermons ended with the anti-smoking coughing song: "Ugge-ugge-ugge-ugge" (in Dutch the guttural "g" sounds exactly like a cough). The Publicity Song followed: "Publicity, publicity, publicity, moooooooooore publicity." Everyone sang along until no one could keep up with the increasing tempo.

Grootveld's rituals were, in a sense, Happenings, and over time they became increasingly frenzied. On April 18th, 1964, he burned down the shed, which he was now calling the Church for Aware Nicotine Addicts. While setting the gasoline-soaked newspapers aflame he cried: "Remember Van Der Lubbe!" (It was a reference to the Dutchman accused of burning the German Reichstag in 1933, an incident that consolidated Nazi power.) At first his audience thought it was a joke, but they fled the premises once they realized what was happening and Grootveld was arrested by the police. In court he testified that he hadn't meant to burn down his temple, it was a case of "a ritual that got out of hand." For this particular performance he was placed on probation.

Despite his probation, Grootveld continued his Happenings. For an exhibition of 31 anti-smoking paintings at the LSD Gallery on the Prinsengracht Canal, he arrived at the opening in a rubber raft. In a speech, he advanced the thesis that millions of people, the tobacco addicts, were human burnt offerings to the totems of advertising and the tobacco companies that profited from them. He facetiously included marijuana, pills, and opium as part of the problem, inverting the famous *Communist Manifesto* quote by stating: "Opium is the religion of our people." He insisted that the only weapon he had to oppose the millions spent by the tobacco industry was *een ietsie-bietsie exhibietsie* (meaning "some itsy-bitsy exhibition").

Grootveld's word-play and punning were masterful, though they can only be fully appreciated in Dutch. Since one of his goals was to sow chaos among the police, who had been conducting arrests for possession of marijuana, he next launched the "Marihu" project, "marihu" being short for marijuana in its Dutch spelling (marihuana). Employing the Dutch phonetic system of spelling, he concocted a series of puns: "Marie what? Marie where? Marihu! Watch out for the Mariheer!" (the Marihuana Master). Defining marihu as anything that smoked, including straw, wood, weeds, and marijuana — but never tobacco! — he designed a Marihuette game patterned after Russian Roulette. The rules for the game appeared as a manifesto, "Marihu #2," which Grootveld called a magic chain letter and requested that people copy five times and circulate among their friends. The chain-letter strategy gave his followers the freedom of improving on or adding to the rules at the same time as they learned the game. And it was in the Marihu manifesto that the city of Amsterdam was first identified as "The Magic Center."

"Marihu #2" instructed everyone to make packages of marihu and get them into circulation. Grootveld's names for the various marihu substances were puns in Dutch, French, and English, such as marivoodoo, marivoodoomari, maritaboo, mariboobytrap, mariyoghurt and marihuwelijk (a pun on the Dutch word for wedding, "huwelijk," a word Provo would soon charge with political connotations). The puns were often at the expense of brand names for Dutch cigarettes and various aspects of Dutch society. They often rhymed and caught on easily in Amsterdam.

Grootveld claimed that everything was marihu and marihu was everywhere. On the absurd chance that the game generated profits, he averred that they would be turned over to the *Consumptiebond*, which is a Dutch pun on "Consumer's Organization" also meaning "Tuberculosis Organization," a disease gravely affected by smoking. He filled hundreds of empty cigarette packets with the marihu substances, and whenever he saw someone buying a pack of cigarettes from an automatic vending machine he asked the person to keep the drawer open so he could insert a packet of marihu. He was becoming a well-known figure and Amsterdammers have a taste for both humor and political adventure, so people would often oblige him. They understood that the next automat patron would be purchasing a packet of marihu.

Though there were countless participants, no one fully understood the rules for Marihuette. The game had a point system: a marijuana bust (or arrest) was 100 points; a voluntary visit to the police station was 150 points, and so on. But the system grew hopelessly elaborate when Marihuette players began informing the police of their actions as part of the points system. In one celebrated incident, tipping the police came full circle to strike Grootveld. Fred Wessels, the painter who in 1963 held the Ice Happening in his home in the Jordaan, had an exhibition of anti-smoking paintings opening in Dendermonde, Belgium. A group of 20 supporters, including Grootveld and Bart Huges, set out from Amsterdam to attend. Acting on information from the Dutch police, the Belgian police arrested them at the border — Grootveld himself had tipped a friendly policeman about the group's itinerary. A large quantity of marihu was confiscated, but since none of it included actual marijuana no arrests were made. Recognizing that total chaos had set in, the Dutch police gave up their attempts to bust marihu users.

In Grootveld's view, the nonsense manifested in the marihu game mimicked an absurdity he observed in real life. Addicted potheads were being arrested by nicotine-addicted policemen, and the incidents were being reported by alcoholic journalists and read in the press or viewed on television by a public addicted to cigarettes and consumerism.

Following the success of the Marihu game, Grootveld's *Acetone Miep* performance aimed to interfere directly with tobacco retailers. He cross-dressed as a woman and entered tobacco shops. Asking to use the telephone, he then dropped a bottle of acetone on the floor allowing the fumes from the chemical to fill the store, robbing the tobacco of its taste as it settled on the merchandise.

The Acetone Miep campaign led to constant arrests, but Grootveld was undeterred. He expanded his actions to include other issues. By helping his friend Aad Veldhoen market his erotic prints from the bakfiets Grootveld had used to cycle to Paris, the two dealt directly with the public, bypassing the commercialized art gallery scene. (It is interesting to note that, like Grootveld, Aad Veldhoen is now considered a Dutch national treasure.) They initiated their project at the *Lieverdje* (pronounced Lee-Vert-Cheh and meaning "the beloved little one"), the statue of a small boy located in a street called *Het Spui* (pronounced, approximately, Spow) near the Leidseplein. The statue was meant to be an expression of Amsterdam's desire to honor someone besides a general or a monarch, but Grootveld had noticed that there was a bronze plaque on the pedestal stating that it was a gift to the city of Amsterdam from the Hunter Tobacco Company. Grootveld and Veldhoen sold the prints for a week before the police stepped in, judging three nudes unfit for viewing by minors, and the two entrepreneurs were fined eleven guilders for each picture.

Though the charges were later dropped, Grootveld turned his immediate anger towards the little statue and its donor, furious that it was dedicated to what he characterized as "the addicted consumer of the future." To protest its presence he organized gatherings at the Lieverdje every Saturday at midnight, giving speeches that always ended with a burnt offering. The police often interfered, but Grootveld persisted. Dozens of teenagers and university students began showing up, chanting "Image, Image" in the French pronunciation (Ee-Ma-Jeh) and shouting some of Grootveld's slogans, including the coughing chant: "Ugge, ugge." Grootveld would then conduct a solemn sermon against smoking: "Friends, we are gathered here in this earliest hour on Sunday..."

The ritual Happenings at the Lieverdje, which began in June 1964, continued until September 1965, interrupted only by bad weather and police interference. At these, Grootveld extended his attack on the advertising network of publication and publicity, calling upon people to "name the names" in the vast computer system that controls and directs modern life. He laid blame for Western culture's addictive tendencies at the feet of the dope syndicates, by which he meant the tobacco industry, the liquor industry, the media and all media advertising, and the nauseating middle class (*het misselijk makende middenstand*). He predicted a future where the press would become so corrupt and bland that illegal newspapers would spring up everywhere. He envisioned a special mission for the city of Amsterdam, describing the extraordinary effects the encircling pattern of the canals had on him. He predicted, quite prophetically, that a mass influx of young people, particularly from America, would soon arrive in Amsterdam, and that the "Publicity," the image, of the city would prove an irresistible magnet.

Although the Happenings Grootveld staged at the Lieverdje supplied the form, it was another of his ideas that ignited the atmosphere that gave birth to Provo. At rituals he continued at his burned-out temple, Grootveld predicted that the world's prophets would soon gather in Amsterdam. And as the middle class moved

The Lieverdje statue set afire (at one of the Happenings).

to new housing outside the old center of the city, the vacant buildings in the city center would provide housing for the new prophets of the Magic Center. (This proved to be an uncanny forecast of plans that the anarchist Kabouter (pronounced Kab-Out-Er) movement developed for Amsterdam's vacant and condemned buildings six years later, plans that propelled the emergence of Amsterdam's squatting movement.) Grootveld's collective term for the arriving prophets was *Klaas*, short for Saint Nicholas (familiarly called Sinter Klaas and adopted in the English-speaking world as Santa Claus) the patron saint of Amsterdam. In his view, a Council of Klaases would resolve the vacuum in society created by the corruption of modern civilization. Although Grootveld didn't know who the Klaas figurehead would be, Amsterdam's metamorphosis into the Magic Center would be resolved dialectically because the Klaas who appeared would be an impoverished and impotent exhibitionist. This confusing prophetic vision led to a new campaign. In place of chalking up K for cancer, he took to chalking walls and advertising with the slogan "*Klaas kom!*" ("Claus is Coming!") Grootveld preached. "Claus must come. Claus will come! Claus is the new prophet!"

works referenced

Duyn (1967c); Meier (1966); Reeuwijk (1965).

3. the birth of provo (may–july 1965)

And Klaas came!

As Harry Mulisch, a leading Dutch novelist and essayist, noted, "Klaas came and was called Claus." His full name was Claus Von Amsberg, a 37-year-old German diplomat and member of the minor German nobility who at the age of 17 had served in the German Army alongside the other boys Hitler conscripted at the end of the war to defend the fatherland. This otherwise-obscure foreigner was catapulted to fame overnight by virtue of becoming the fiancé of Princess Beatrix, the oldest of Queen Juliana's four daughters and heiress to the Dutch throne. The official announcement of the engagement came on June 28, 1965 as the much-awaited climax of a hectic seven-week period of wild speculation and veiled disclosure. And with his "Claus is Coming!" prophecy realized, Grootveld's prestige soared to new heights. It now seemed as if the stage had been set and the actors were being prompted by fate to speak their lines.

Because she was single and 27, there had been much media speculation about Beatrix's future. The Dutch government is responsible for the succession to the throne, and initially the politicians handled her engagement to Claus Von Amsberg secretively, which only inflamed the negative sentiments they wished to keep dormant. In 1964, Beatrix's younger sister Irene had married Prince Charles Hugues de Bourbon-Parma, a pretender to the then-vacant Spanish throne. Irene's union had been unpopular because of widespread aversion to the fascist regime of Generalissimo Franco, and it was unacceptable to the Dutch law of succession because it necessitated her conversion to Catholicism. The Dutch royal family, the House of Oranje (pronounced Oh-Ran-Yeh, meaning "orange"), is required by "constitutional tradition" to belong to the Protestant Dutch Reformed Church, a historical holdover from the Netherlands' successful struggle for independence against Catholic Spain in the 16th century. Irene's secret conversion became public when

The founding of Provo. Roel van Duyn is in the stripped shirt and Rob Stolk is wearing a checkered shirt and sitting on a bicycle. Taken in front of Karthuizersstraat, 14 where Van Duyn and Stolk rented apartments.

she was photographed praying in a Catholic church in Denmark. As a result, she was forced to officially renounce all rights to the Dutch throne on behalf of herself and her heirs.

Ironically, it was a coalition government dominated by the Catholic People's Party (KVP) that delivered this demand. Constitutional tradition was at odds with the reality of the country's demographics. As a result of a declining Protestant birthrate and large Catholic families, Catholicism had become the largest religious denomination in the country, comprising 40% of the population. But the Catholics lived in a nation that identified itself as Protestant by virtue of both tradition and economic domination. In the early 1960s a tense atmosphere prevailed between Protestants and Catholics, but as a result of the changing ecumenical climate in world Christianity and the breakdown of the Zuilen system, the 1977 national elections in the Netherlands would see the merger of the two major Protestant political parties with the Catholic People's Party into the new *Christiaan Demokratisch Appel* (CDA).

However, in the more conservative climate of 1965, Irene's wedding had put Beatrix in a delicate position. Despite the government's best efforts at discretion, on May 6th the sensationalist English tabloid *Daily Express* published photographs of Princess Beatrix walking arm-in-arm with an "unidentified" young man. The photos were taken by a Dutch freelance photographer named John De Rooij, who snuck onto the grounds of Beatrix's private castle, *Drakensteyn*, and they appeared the next day in *De Telegraaf*, a salacious Dutch tabloid that was about to play a prominent role in the emerging history of the Provo movement. Rumors of Beatrix's engagement to an "ex-Nazi" named Claus Von Amsberg only a year after Irene's unpopular marriage and abdication was a political bombshell. Still, even after the photograph appeared in the press, no announcement was forthcoming from the royal family. In the tense weeks that followed, the entire country awaited word of confirmation.

The political establishment in the Netherlands was a complex structure that never challenged the political grounds of the marriage, but the moderate Left began tearing itself to pieces as it tried to decide which position to take. Unfortunately, as the next two years would show, both the Socialist and Communist parties had integrated themselves deeply into the establishment years earlier. Though the two leading socialist papers, *Het Parool* and *Het Vrije Volk*, were critical of the marriage, the Dutch Socialist Party, Partij van de Arbeid, claimed that the papers did not reflect the official position of the party itself. The steering committee of the National Federative Council of the Former Resistance Movement in the Netherlands said that it would refrain from taking a position on the marriage, but six prominent members of the wartime resistance issued a statement deploring it. In their case, opposition was made on grounds of royal succession rather than on issues of personality. They felt that Beatrix ought to abdicate her right to the throne when she married Claus Von Amsberg simply because of the sinister implications of his Nazi past. Indeed, Von Amsberg was a personable, capable, and attractive man who was generally well liked, even by people who objected politically to him becoming the future Prince Consort.

By June 1965, leaders of the five major political parties in the *Tweede Kamer*, which is the lower house of the Dutch parliament (much like the House of Commons in Great Britain or the Assemblee Nationale in France), issued press statements that sanctioned the marriage. Any hesitancy on the part of any particular party was masked by the Tweede Kamer's polite acceptance of Beatrix's choice. It was this tacit consent that the Catholic-dominated coalition government had worked for behind closed doors, and the secretive manner that they found expedient at the time set the tone for handling all questions relating to the monarchy in 1965. However, the secrecy that passed for expediency would soon demonstrate that the government was deeply alienated from a significant sector of the Dutch people.

After sanctioning the marriage, the government confidently submitted a Bill of Consent for the marriage and a Bill of Naturalization for Claus Von Amsberg to the Tweede Kamer. Only the small Pacifist-Socialist Party remained unequivocally opposed, as it was to the continued existence of the monarchy. The Dutch Communist Party, at the time a dreary Stalinist backwater with a large following, avoided taking an immediate position. The Communists ultimately abstained from the vote in the Tweede Kamer for reasons of social respectability, claiming to be against undue haste rather than against Von Amsberg's past. The Party leadership remained steadfastly opposed to all republican and anti-monarchist sentiment, eventually lamenting the rise of the Provo movement that the marriage helped to advance. It was probably a source of undying mortification to them that the rank-and-file membership of one of their unions became the spark plug that ignited the greatest riot during the Provo struggle. In 1968 the French Communist Party would conducted itself similarly, to such an extent that the Communists would be credited with the collapse of the May 1968 revolt.

The complex history of the Dutch royal family must be appreciated in order to understand the situation that had begun to unfold. The House of Oranje has been unpopular throughout much of its history, with the exception of Queen Wilhemina, who, while leading a Dutch government in exile in England and personifying resistance to the Nazi invasion of World War II, had single-handedly re-established the popularity of the royal family. Otherwise the dynasty had been tolerated rather than embraced, even in its best hours.

For more than a century, Dutch monarchs have married German royalty and nobility, so the Dutch royal family, like most European royalty, is largely German by blood. During the 1960s, the reigning Queen, Juliana, was something of a retiring, matronly Hausfrau. She was also, incidentally, one of the richest women in the world by virtue of shares the crown owned in Royal Dutch Shell and other companies. Her husband, Bernhard, the Prince-Consort, was a capable, outgoing man active in economic affairs, and a permanent Dutch goodwill ambassador to Latin America because of his fluency in Spanish. Like Von Amsberg, Bernhard was a member of the German petty nobility. He had severed his Nazi affiliations in 1936 when he became engaged to Princess Juliana and served as Commander of the Dutch armed forces-in-exile in England and thus had a "good" war record. Juliana and Bernhard were married in January 1937 and he was made a captain in the Dutch army. Before going into exile, the young couple had moved into the palace at Soestdijk that had been partially modernized as a "gift" from the Dutch people. Nevertheless, rumors about Bernhard's shady business dealings had been circulating for many years, and would resurface in 1976 when the Dutch government conducted hearings on bribes he had taken from the Lockheed Company.

Until 1964, Queen Juliana's reign had been fairly calm. There was only one scandalous episode, in 1956, when a faith healer named Geert Hofmans was retained by the Royal Court to cure the eyesight of the youngest princess, who was almost blind. Miss Hofmans was a dedicated pacifist who managed to exert much influence upon the Queen, which proved a great political embarrassment in the time of the Cold War. Prince Bernhard had her removed. Otherwise, the middle-class decorum of the royal family set a conservative tone for the country's moral and social life, which by 1965 seemed destined to endure forever.

The formal wedding announcement came on June 28, 1965 in the form of a press conference held before several hundred international journalists and photographers. By then public opposition to the marriage and the monarchy was being tempered by a general aversion to the presidential system. In other words, none of the country's professional politicians was an attractive presidential candidate. Characters like the Foreign Minister, Luns, were more disturbing to many people, including the far-left fringe of Amsterdam, than Beatrix or Claus could ever be. Seen in the light of the politics of the time, the republicanist, anti-royalist sentiment that surfaced in 1965–66 was primarily a protest against the Establishment's paternalistic Zuilen system and the conservative tone that the monarchy set for political and social life. At the press conference Princess Beatrix and her fiancé were raked over the coals, but they handled themselves well.

The results of three public opinion polls taken in 1965 indicated that the Dutch population averaged 73% for the marriage, 12% against, and 15% with no opinion. A petition opposing the marriage got a scant 65,000 signatures nationwide. The Bill of Consent to the marriage would pass easily in December 1965. In the Tweede Kamer the vote would be 132–9, with 9 abstentions. In the *Eerste Kamer* (the Upper House), the vote would be 65–5, with 5 abstentions. The Communist Party abstained in both houses. Again, only the small Pacifist-Socialist Party would openly oppose the marriage, joined by a few Socialists. There was little open opposition to the marriage because the government had managed to saddle both the people and parliament in piecemeal fashion. However, the machinations and secrecy that the government employed were forcing political resentment underground, where a smoldering resentment was gradually building.

After their press conference, Beatrix and Claus made quick visits to the major Dutch cities. Only in Amsterdam did they meet demonstrations. On July 4, 1965,* a few anti-Claus leaflets drifted down from a bridge as they passed through the canals of the city by boat. These free-falling pamphlets, which caught and reflected the daylight in their slow descent, marked the first public political activity of the Provo movement. And from that day onward the police were to pay close attention to this new and unknown group.

Princess Beatrix had decided to be married in Amsterdam, the traditional capital of the country, and the Dutch government, one of the most liberal the Netherlands had known up to that time, unwisely accepted her choice. When opposition to holding the ceremony in Amsterdam began to mount, Prime Minister Cals refused to budge from his original decision, feeling that the government's prestige was at stake. Dutch writer Harry Mulisch characterizes this reaction as a "regent mentality" that follows from a paternalistic governing authority that feels no need to answer to the governed. The Nazis had deported most of the city's Jews, 10% of Amsterdam's pre-war population, to certain death in the concentration camps. Among Amsterdammers, that memory and the general memory of the occupation were still bitter ones. Opposition to the marriage began to harden, reflecting popular dissatisfaction with the government's high-handed manner. The three chief rabbis of Amsterdam, speaking on behalf of the Jewish community, refused invitations to the wedding, as did 18 of the 45 members of the Amsterdam *Gemeenteraad*, the city council. Probably a majority of the

*According to whether you read the accounts published by Van Duyn or Mulisch, this date is in dispute. In *Provo* (Van Duyn, 1985, p. 22), which seems to be an updated version of *Het witte gevaar* (1967), Van Duyn gives the date as July 4. Without claiming to be certain of the true chronology, July 4 is the date I choose to use here.

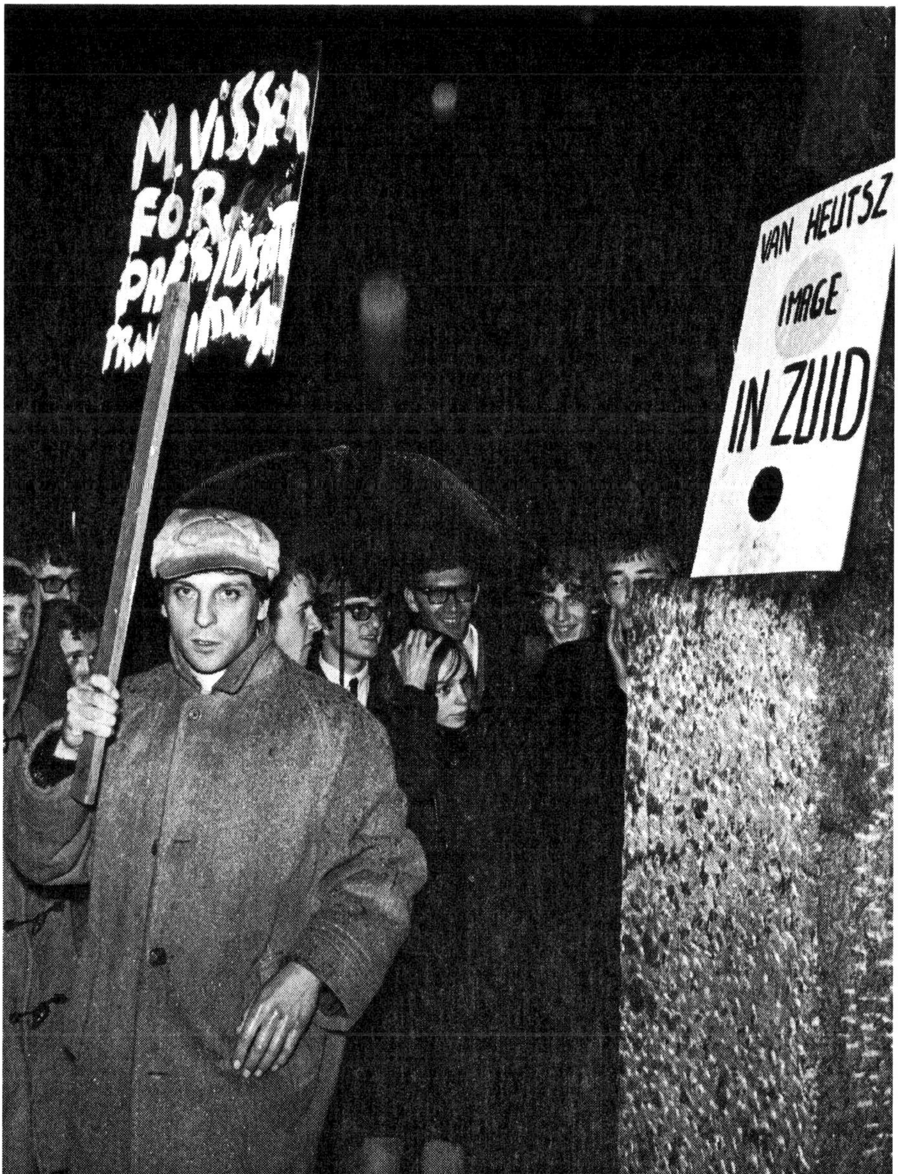

Robert Jasper Grootveld launches the campaign for Maarten Visser for President.

Dutch people, including a majority of Amsterdammers, could have accepted the marriage, despite its political implications and symbolism, but a great many were unwilling to see it held in Amsterdam. Had the marriage taken place elsewhere, say in The Hague, it is unlikely that any rebellion would have taken place.

the birth of provo

Roel Van Duyn, a political theoretician and one of the founders of the Provo movement, was born in The Hague and was 22 at the time of Princess Beatrix's marriage. He had already proven to be a gifted political thinker and an effective activist for pacifist causes, a revolutionary purist and a writer with acute insight into and feeling for people and history. His book, *Het witte gevaar: een vademekum voor Provos (The White Danger: A Handbook for Provos)*, is a major source of information on the movement.

While still in high school in The Hague, Van Duyn had been active in the Ban-The-Bomb Movement. He was dismissed from the progressive Montessori Lyceum after organizing an anti-war sit-in on the busy Laan Van Meerdevoord during rush hour. He also helped organize an anti-war sit-in in Amsterdam that was broken up by the police. When he later enrolled at another high school in The Hague, his fellow students unfurled a banner reading, GO HOME, VAN DUYN. In 1963, he moved to Amsterdam.

During 1964 and early 1965, while still living in Amsterdam, he worked on the staff of the Rotterdam anarchist paper, *De Vrije* (*The Free*), but despite his admiration for the editor found it old-fashioned. He left to start a paper of his own, *Horzel* (*Gadfly*), because in his opinion old-style anarchism in the Netherlands of 1965 couldn't hope to be more than an annoyance to society. He eventually changed the title of his paper after reading a dissertation on the *nozems*, Dutch working-class juvenile delinquents who resembled the English Teddy Boys. *Achtergrond van Nozemgedrag (Background to Nozem Behavior)*, by Wouter Buikhuisen, attracted great attention in the Dutch press at the time of its publication in 1965. Buikhuisen had studied the deliberately provocative anti-social behavior of bored, unemployable teenagers against adult society in the modern welfare state. The nozems shouted obscenities at older people, sometimes even going so far as to shove them off the sidewalks. Buikhuisen called them *provos*, adapting his term from the French word *provoquer*, which means to provoke and is similar to a word in Dutch. Van Duyn responded to the implications of Buikhuisen's analysis by choosing *Provo* as his new title. (During the summer of 1965, as a result of Provo actions against the marriage, Buikhuisen gained national fame. Incorrectly, though perhaps understandably, he was considered both by the press and the government to be an expert on the new Provo movement.)

Van Duyn felt that young Dutch anarchists needed to base their political activity on the revolutionary potential of the nozems by learning to channel aggression into a conscious revolutionary force. In the pages of *Provo* he urged students to become Provos, which is to say revolutionary nozems. Though anarchists could no longer hope for social revolution in the Netherlands, he insisted that they could and should provoke the authorities and the State. This brilliant analytical and political coup provided a major springboard for the "Provolution," and is perhaps Van Duyn's greatest contribution to the Provo movement.

A letter to *De Vrije* in March of 1965 had put Van Duyn in contact with Rob Stolk, who was from Zaandam to the north of Amsterdam. Though only nineteen, Stolk too was a young pacifist activist. (He would subsequently become one of the leading Provos.) Stolk and Van Duyn joined forces to publish *Barst (Burst)*, which ran for only one issue, April 1965, but included an open letter from "pre-Provo" Garmt Kroeze to the B.V.D. (the Dutch FBI) stating that they, the anarchists/Provos, would "burst the smooth façade of a society that debases human beings by turning them into machines of conspicuous consumption." The burst façade would bring about the collapse of middle-class society.

Provo formally announced itself in a stenciled leaflet dated May 25th, 1965 and signed by Van Duyn, Martijn Lindt, and Robert Hartzema (the latter two using pseudonyms). The leaflet criticized the existing pacifist movement for not accomplishing the job that needed to be done and for having reduced itself to an annual protest march in Amsterdam "staged with painful regularity." It announced that the Provos would abandon empty gestures in favor of more provocative modes of action, undertaking a last desperate effort to change society, even if that effort was doomed to failure. Several Dutch commentators later called this the most pessimistic manifesto of birth made by a modern political movement, but noted that events of the coming year turned Van Duyn into an eager optimist. The optimism lay in the manifesto's claim that Provo would bring about the rebirth of anarchism, creating an aware new generation and becoming a new source of inspiration for political activism.

> Dear Comrades,
>
> The anti-Bomb movement, which seemed to be the only dynamic element on the Left in Holland, has disappeared up a back alley. The ban-the-bomb groups have given up their work.
>
> The "November 29 Committee" hardly functions any more and just acts occasionally without any real conviction.

Robert Jasper Grootveld and Rob Stolk. Probably at the Lieverdje.

The Peace Committee and the People's Committee do not seem to be able to attract many more supporters and are becoming isolated.

The annual march through Amsterdam, performed with the painful regularity and senselessness of a ritual, only just manages to keep the flame burning.

The Dutch Left will have to find new ways of achieving real results before it loses its attraction altogether. We believe that non-violent dissidence is only incidentally appropriate to our ends because it is not happening on a large scale.

When slogans and gestures fail we have to turn to action and attack. We believe that only a revolutionary Left movement can bring about change!

This preference for direct action leads us to anarchist concepts. Anarchism propagates the most direct rebellion against all authority, whether it be democratic or communist.

The Dutch anarchist movement has been languishing since the war. We want to renew anarchism and spread the word, especially among the younger generation.

How? Through *PROVO*, which will appear monthly starting July 1965.

PROVO is a new magazine — as if there weren't enough already. However, it's the only one radically opposed to this society. Why?

> - Because this capitalist society is poisoning itself with a morbid thirst for money. Its members are being brought up to worship Having and despise Being.
>
> - Because this bureaucratic society is choking itself with officialdom and suppressing any form of spontaneity. Its members can only become creative, individual people through anti-social conduct.
>
> - Because this militaristic society is digging its own grave by a paranoid arms build-up. Its members now have nothing to look forward to but certain death by atomic radiation.

PROVO feels it must make a choice: desperate revolt or cowering defeat. PROVO encourages rebellion wherever it can. PROVO knows it must be the loser in the end, but it cannot miss the chance to thoroughly provoke this society once more.

PROVO sees anarchism as a well of inspiration for the revolt. PROVO wants to renew anarchism and bring it to the young.

Our issues will contain material which is varied, up-to-the-minute, and provocative to the ruling class, and we'll also regularly publish issues devoted to special subjects. On the agenda we have:

- What is anarchism?
- de Sade
- Dada
- Militarism and the Dutch army
- Prostitution
- Revolt and conditions in the Jordaan
- Etc.

PROVO will take the initiative in all kinds of direct action. *PROVO* wants to gather around it a core of anarchist youth. *PROVO* is eager to co-operate with all other anarchist groups.

In addition, *PROVO* will regularly issue pamphlets entitled *PROVOkaties* No. 1, 2, 3, etc.

GIVE US A CHANCE!

None of this will be realized without your help. We desperately need several hundred guilders to set up *PROVO*. For us penniless students the cost of printing the first issue, plus postage, advertising, manifestos, etc., is far too much.

So we ask you kindly but PROVOcatively: send a large sum of money without delay to our administrative address, Karthuizerstraat 14, Amsterdam C.

The Editorial Board
25 May, 1965
(From *BAMN*, translation used with permission)

The first of the promised *Provokaties* (*Provocations*) soon followed the Provo manifesto. It was entitled *Goed dat er politie is... (Good That There Are Police...)* and failed to capture public attention. But *Provokatie #2*, *Claus Von Amsberg, Persona Non Grata*, hit the mark. Olaf Stoop, a member of the core Provo group, slipped it into copies of the conservative newspaper *De Telegraaf* that he sold at a newsstand in Amsterdam's Schipol Airport. Stoop was fired as a result but his guerilla action finally got the name of Provo in print, gaining necessary publicity for the fledgling movement.

Van Duyn was aware of Grootveld's Saturday night rituals at the Lieverdje. He often attended and found them "uniquely creative," completely different from anything else going on in Amsterdam at that time. According to him, Grootveld was responsible for preparing Amsterdam's youth for the emergence of Provo by introducing the street Happening to the Leidseplein crowd and supplying much of the new vocabulary and symbolism that Provo adopted. In late May, at one of the Lieverdje Happenings, Van Duyn and Stolk passed out the leaflets announcing their forthcoming anarchist periodical, *Provo*. Grootveld invited them to his apartment because he was interested in the new magazine. He told them that his father had been an anarchist and explained that Amsterdam was the Magic Center from which the *Klazen* (Clauses) would launch their mission. He invited the Provos to work with him.

Meanwhile, the police and the Amsterdam city officials remained anxious to quell any protest of Beatrix's engagement, and the atmosphere in the city became increasingly repressive. Though the mayor, Gijsbert Van Hall, was a nominal Socialist, he occupied his position at the Queen's (i.e., the National Government's) discretion. The Amsterdam police force was under his control, but he was personally accountable to the national Ministry of the Interior rather than the Amsterdam City Council. Van Hall's implacable rigidity at the beginning of the political opposition to the coming royal marriage set the tone for the official response to the events that would unfold over the following months.

"Provocation No. 10"—a Provo flyer. Translation: If you see a car emitting lots of poisonous gas, take its number and phone 81206 between 4:30 and 5. Provo will move into action—and we know how to deal with them!

On the evening of July 3rd, a group of seven people protested the visit of Princess Beatrix and Claus Von Amsberg planned for the next day by laying a wreath of flowers at the National Monument on the Dam (the central Square of Amsterdam). Instead of letting this small demonstration run its course, Mayor Van Hall chose to have the seven arrested. He also ordered his police to harass the many Amsterdammers who flew their Dutch flags at half-mast the next day as Beatrix and Claus toured the city.

For their part, the Provos were likewise moving towards confrontation. On July 3rd several of them met at the Lieverdje with copies of *Provokatie #3*, *Which of the Three?* — referring to Prince Bernhard, the husband of Queen Juliana; Don Carlos (Prince Charles Hugues de Bourbon-Parma), the husband of Princess Irene; and Claus Von Amsberg. The ironic question posed by the title was: Which of the three was the most democratic? It was answered with a brief review of each man's allegedly fascist background. This was the pamphlet dropped from the bridge into the *rondvaartboot* (glass-top touring boat) in which Princess Beatrix and Claus toured the city.

Provokatie #3 was designed for trouble. The pamphlet included a newspaper photograph of Prince Bernhard that had been copyrighted by the firm of Stevens & Magielsen. The firm sued the Provos for copyright violation, and Van Duyn was charged a fine plus legal costs, which came to 530 guilders (about U.S.$148 in 1965 dollars), which was not inconsequential for a penniless Provo. Afterwards the leaflet was reissued with the word *censuur* (censored) in place of the photograph.

Instead of showing up in court, Van Duyn sent a note stating it was "simply impossible to hold one single individual responsible. Provo is the product of an ever-changing, anonymous gang of subversive elements.... Provo doesn't recognize copyright, as it is just another form of private property which is renounced by Provo.... We suspect that this is an indirect form of censorship while the State is too cowardly to sue us straight for *lese majeste* an offense violating the dignity of the ruler.... By the way, our hearts are filled with a general contempt for authorities and for anyone who submits himself to them."

Provokatie #3 was the first of many Provo publications seized by the Amsterdam police. In *The White Danger* Van Duyn lists the following publications as having been confiscated: issues 1 and 7 of *Provo*, Provokaties 3, 7, 9 and 13, three unnumbered leaflets, two issues of *Image*, and two issues of *God, Nederland en Oranje*. The charges against *Provokatie #3* were copyright violation for using the photo of Prince Bernhart, and publishing inflammatory material.

The first issue of *Provo* finally appeared on July 12th, 1965. The magazine was both the nucleus of the movement and the most tangible proof of its existence. It called for revolutionizing the nozems of Amsterdam's central area, *Het Centrum*. The article that resulted in the magazine's notorious bust was entitled "The Practical Anarchist," a reprint from an old anarchist magazine from around 1900 that advocated the use of dynamite to achieve the goals of social reform. It argued that the life of one anarchist was worth that of a hundred capitalists. To add zest to the article, considered by the Provos to be a joke, the kind of cap used in a cap gun was placed in the text with instructions on how to make it explode. The police seizure of *Provo #1* was a tremendous publicity stunt. Both the police and the State had been provoked! Under the constant, if not tender, attention of the police, over the next eight months the Provo group was to grow from about 50 loosely associated individuals to more than 5,000 activists and sympathizers.

De Telegraaf was the first newspaper to anticipate the Provo "menace." On July 24th, journalist Conny Sluysmans published an interview with eight of the Provos. In her commentary she noted that they had long hair for the most part, wore torn clothing, and were aged 16 to 33. She described them as young people who refused to work and were opposed to everything. They smoked marijuana and attended Grootveld's Saturday night Happenings. She complained that none of them offered to open the door for her when she concluded the interview. She concurred with the opinion of an informant who knew them and had called them a "bunch of degenerates."

In his recollection of the interview, Van Duyn mentions claiming that Provo was rooted not in the working class but in the loafing class. He explained that thanks to media publicity a handful of anarchist provocateurs were considered to be a segment of the population, whereas the truth was that all they had really done was to effectively reveal the great unrest hidden beneath the surface of society's smooth veneer.

works referenced

Banning (1966); Berg (1967); Buikhuizen (1965); Van Duyn (1967c); Hofland (1972); Mulisch (1967); Rooij (1966); Singer (1970); Stansill and Mairowitz (1998); Voeten (1990).

VAN
'S-GRAVENHAGE

Aan Postbus 1602

te Amsterdam

Hiermede verzoek ik U voor rekening van de Gemeentepolitie van 's-Gravenhage de onderstaande goederen te leveren c.q. werkzaamheden te verrichten.

	f
1 abonnement op het blad"Provo" m.i.v. 1-10-'66	
	f

Bezorgadres: Gemeente Politie
Postbus 264
'S-GRAVENHAGE.

Rekening in duplo in te dienen bij het bureau comptabiliteit der Gemeentepolitie van 's-Gravenhage. Postbus 264. No. BESTELBON OP REKENING VERMELDEN.

Pol. 721

's-Gravenhage, 30-9 1966
DE HOOFDCOMMISSARIS VAN POLITIE,
namens deze,
DE CHEF INKOOP

(G. J. van de Waal.)

Politie neemt blaadje in beslag

Provo cartoon by Willem.

4. the state is provoked! (july 1965–march 1966)

The thesis of provocation was to prove a huge success, and a major component of its success lay in the unwitting but indispensable participation of the government. Essentially, with limited means, the Provos managed to dupe the Dutch government into bringing in heavy artillery to kill a fly. And the fly somehow managed to orchestrate the ensuing events to its own best advantage. The government was provoked! And it swallowed the bait! But the factor that might have really ensured government involvement may have been that the Provos were self-proclaimed anarchists, so their anti-monarchist position led the authorities to fear that a Provo or someone indirectly influenced by the Provos might attempt to assassinate a member of the Royal Family.

The first confrontation between the police and the Provos took place over an innocent presentation on the ecology of the automobile: the White Bicycle Plan. The plan was authored by Provo Luud Schimmelpennick, an industrial designer and future member of the rotating Provo seat on the Amsterdam city council. It was the first of the celebrated White Plans that comprised the Provo political platform.

Provokatie #5
PROVO's Bicycle Plan

Amsterdammers!

The asphalt terror of the motorized bourgeoisie has lasted long enough. Human sacrifices are made daily to this latest idol of the idiots: car power. Choking carbon monoxide is its incense, its image contaminates thousands of canals and streets.

PROVO's bicycle plan will liberate us from the car monster. PROVO introduces the WHITE BICYCLE, a piece of public property.

The first white bicycle will be presented to the Press and public on Wednesday July 28 at 3 P.M. near the statue of the Lieverdje, the addicted consumer, on the Spui.

The white bicycle is never locked. The white bicycle is the first free communal transport. The white bicycle is a provocation against capitalist private property, for THE WHITE BICYCLE IS ANARCHISTIC.

The white bicycle can be used by anyone who needs it and then must be left for someone else. There will be more and more white bicycles until everyone can use white transport and the car peril is past. The white bicycle is a symbol of simplicity and cleanliness in contrast to the vanity and foulness of the authoritarian car. In other words:

A BIKE IS SOMETHING, BUT ALMOST NOTHING!

(From BAMN, translation used with permission.)

The Provos hailed the plan as a protest against private property and a free means of public transport, boasting that unlike the buses and trams it never closed. Borrowing their imagery from Robert Jasper Grootveld, they spoke of automobiles as the asphalt terror of the middle class. The consuming masses paid homage to the auto-authority, for whom carbon monoxide was an incense, while the casualties of automobile accidents were its daily sacrificial victims. The closing remark, "*Immers een fiets is iets, maar bijna niets*" (a bicycle is always something, but almost nothing), was a reference to how much less space a bicycle occupies than an automobile does, as well as to the fact that bicycles don't pollute the atmosphere. At the time, many Dutch people used bicycles as their only means of transport, so an automobile was obviously much more a consumer status symbol than an absolute necessity.

On Tuesday night, July 27th, Olaf Stoop and Dick Roseboom were arrested for posting copies of *Provokatie #5* throughout the city. The next day the first white bicycles were presented to a crowd at the Lieverdje. Grootveld held forth on the asphalt terror of the motorized masses (*asfalt-terreur van het gemotoriseerde klootjesvolk*). Behind him, several Provos busily painted black bicycles white. The police were present, but no one was arrested. One officer told a reporter that no one would be arrested as long as automobile traffic was not obstructed.

Four days later, on Saturday, July 31st, another crowd gathered at the Lieverdje to witness Grootveld's regular midnight ritual. But Grootveld didn't show, so as a way of honoring his absence his followers set fire to a stack of newspapers at the foot of the Lieverdje statue and began to chant, "Image, Image!" and other slogans based on Grootveld's puns. The Provos, few strays that they were, continued the work of painting bicycles white. Then a white police Volkswagen pulled up, discharging four policemen who surrounded the Lieverdje statue and ordered the crowd to disperse. Van

Duyn, who was painting a bicycle, was ordered to move out. When he asked why, a policeman struck him with a club. His girlfriend dragged him to safety, but the crowd refused to disperse. Sensing that they were helpless and outnumbered, the police returned to their Volkswagen and drove off. Traffic at the busy intersection came to a halt. The "Holy Cows," as the Provos had taken to calling automobiles, began to moo (honk), but the Lieverdje crowd held its ground.

Direct provocation of the police was the earliest and most effective Provo tactic. The Provos had intuited that exploitation of the "fascistic" regent mentality of the police might just be provocative enough to transform Provo from a small passionate and gifted nucleus of politically frustrated individuals into an effective and expanding political movement. During the following months, as the police beat up both innocent bystanders and demonstrators, the use of intemperate violence would galvanize much of Amsterdam's population in support of the anarchists' right to hold Happenings. Using the metaphors of chemistry, we can view the police as a catalytic agent, the catalyst remaining unchanged even as it produces a chemical reaction. In fact, the police soon became almost the sole agent in generating political polarization in Amsterdam.

On July 28th, when the first white bicycles became publicly available, Police Commissioner Landman had promised that there would be no arrests. However, the police didn't adhere to his policy. Soon they were confiscating white bicycles throughout the city, justifying their action with the circular reasoning that the bicycles were not locked and therefore invited theft, which, of course, is prohibited by law. Some 50 white bicycles were confiscated. "*Polietsie, polietsie, waar is m'n fietsie?*" (Policemen, policemen, where is my bicycle?) became the new Provo cry at the Lieverdje. Ironically, while the police accused the Provos of blocking traffic with their bicycle Happenings, the White Bicycle Plan was meant as a solution to Amsterdam's increasing traffic congestion.

The Provos had been quick to see the basic injustice of owning a private automobile in the crowded living conditions of Western Europe. The technical and theoretical justification for the White Bicycle Plan was laid out by its originator, Luud Schimmelpennick, in *Provo #2* (August 17, 1965). He noted that in 1634 the burgemeesters of Amsterdam hadn't allowed carriages into the city because the streets were too narrow. At that point in history, six parking lots had been laid out at the main entrances to the city, one of which was, symbolically enough, the Leidseplein. Passengers had to leave their vehicles in the lots and enter the city on foot. Schimmelpennick's plan made it clear that it was the 7% of rush-hour commuters who drove automobiles who truly created the congestion for streetcars, bicycles, and pedestrians and polluted the air. Furthermore, 71.4% of all traffic victims were pedestrians "sacrificed to the Holy automobile." To solve the problems Schimmelpennick made the following suggestions: close the center of Amsterdam to motor vehicles; have the city of Amsterdam purchase 20,000 white bicycles annually to supplement public transportation; allow Provo volunteers to paint anyone's bicycle white at the Lieverdje every Saturday at midnight; have electrically powered municipal taxis; and place parking lots on the outskirts of the city where people could leave their cars and transfer to public transportation.

The White Bicycle Plan was endorsed by the press and enthusiastically received by the Municipal Planning Service of Amsterdam, which claimed it would go a long way toward solving traffic problems in the center of the city. The Provos tried to interest bicycle manufacturers in it and Schimmelpennick worked to design a cheap new bicycle model. As a concession to the police rhetoric about theft, all the plan bicycles would be provided with a lock for which there would be a common key.

The Provos wanted to continue their Happenings at the Lieverdje without the police transforming them into riots every Saturday night. After police raids on July 31st and August 7th, they wrote a letter to the Police Chief, Van der Molen, requesting a meeting. The letter was signed by Grootveld, Schimmelpennick, Van Duyn, and Stolk, and the request was granted. On the afternoon of Saturday, August 14th, Grootveld, Van Duyn, and Stolk met with four police commissioners: Van der Molen, Molenkamp, Landman, and Kessler. In a classic instance of miscommunication, Van der Molen spoke of the responsibility of the police to maintain order, Grootveld gave an anti-smoking speech, and Van Duyn defended the right to hold "illegal demonstrations." The only positive result seemed to come when Van der Molen agreed not to interfere with the Happening that evening if the Provos managed to avoid confronting the police. Despite this promise, at 10:30 P.M. thirty-four police officers encircled the Lieverdje.

At midnight, when Rob Stolk and Garmt Kroeze advanced to lay flowers at the base of the statue, they were immediately arrested. Grootveld arrived shortly afterwards and tried to disperse the crowd of approximately 2,000 people by leading it through the city in a Silent Procession called the *Stille Omgang*, an Amsterdam Catholic tradition. But the crowd refused to move. Instead, they stood their ground and glared at the police. And when a group of nozems threw cans at them, the police charged the crowd and made thirteen arrests. Of the thirteen, four had nothing to do with Provo and were just hanging around. Nevertheless, all thirteen ended up serving sentences of between one and two months in jail.

After this there was another unsuccessful meeting with the city government, this time between Grootveld and Mayor Van Hall. But a combination of police attitudes, sensationalism in the press, and public fascination set the scene for what unfolded next. The Dutch press began to play up the Saturday night Happenings as major confrontations, with one newspaper, the *Algemene Handelsblad*, even suggesting that they might well become a major tourist attraction. When the police showed up at the Lieverdje on August 21st, they had dogs on hand for the first time. Though there was no confrontation that night, Van Duyn speculated that August 28th might see the last of the "classical genre Happenings." However, it rained on the 28th and very few people showed up. Even the police didn't bother to show. Provo Peter Bronkhorst led the ritual, which lasted for thirty minutes, the usual length of one of Grootveld's ritual performances. It was all over by 12:30 A.M.

Shortly afterwards, in an interview with the weekly newspaper *Vrij Nederland*, Carel Kenulmans, the sculptor of the Lieverdje statue, complained about the Provos defacing his sculpture. He suggested that they hold their protest Happenings at the monument to General Van Heutsz, the military "pacifier" of the former Dutch East Indies (now Indonesia) whose memorial is in fashionable South Amsterdam. Given the respective nature of the two monuments, with the Van Heutsz statue representing Dutch imperialism, the Provos followed his suggestion. Beginning on September 4th, three Happenings took place at the new location. They all began at the Lieverdje, where hundreds of people met to parade through the streets for about a mile to the Van Heutsz Monument. Then, after a few speeches, the monument was smeared with white paint and slogans. On September 18th, Peter Bronkhorst and Auke Boersma mounted the statue and refused to come down. The police dispersed the crowd of 200 people and arrested both Provos. This ended the Happenings staged at the Van Heutsz Monument, but the field of action had grown.

The Dutch monarch's annual mid-September *Troonrede* (Throne Speech) to Parliament in The Hague is the Dutch equivalent to the American President's "State of the Union" address. Before the Troonrede of 1965, Hans Tuynman addressed an open letter to the Queen as "Mrs. Von Lippe-Biesterfeld von Mecklenburg." Tuynman was later to write the interesting book *Full-Time Provo* (which is in Dutch but has an English title), and the address he used was an obvious play on both the Queen's German marriage and her German ancestry. In the letter he invited the Queen to join him in public debate in front of the royal palace on the Lange Voorhout in The Hague. Although Queen Juliana didn't appear for the debate, about one hundred Provos arrived carrying a cardboard TV set with a picture of the Queen on it and the word *Image* emblazoned under the picture. The high point of the event came when the chemical-soaked TV was set on fire, producing a column of smoke 30 feet high. At this point the police arrived to disperse the crowd, beating up several people, including an English tourist.

Roel van Duyn had drafted a Troonrede "as it ought to be given" as *Provokatie* #7, which was distributed during and after the event in The Hague. Van Duyn's "Queen" proclaimed the Social Revolution, abolished private property, and urged the workers to seize the means of production, the factories in which they worked. She also offered to abdicate her throne and donate her fortune to the establishment of communes, opening all her palaces to the people in order to alleviate the severe housing shortage in the Netherlands. As a final gesture of goodwill, Queen Juliana pledged her adherence and that of her daughter, Crown Princess Beatrix, to the principles of anarchism and the Provos.

Burning the Queen in effigy and translating her speech into PROVO-speak were the Provos' most audacious acts to date. The police responded by arresting nine Provos for distributing *Provokatie* #7 and confiscating hundreds of copies of the tract. Fortunately, one of the Provos was released early and was able to warn Van Duyn of an impending search of his home in Amsterdam, giving him time to hide the manuscript of the pseudo Throne Speech before the police arrived. Their search turned up little except some rusty stenciling equipment, and they left without finding anything compromising on the premises. Nevertheless, the pressure was on.

The police were now prepared to believe anything that might lead to the arrest of a Provo. Rob Stolk lived upstairs from Van Duyn. Towards the end of September, two policemen stormed Stolk's room on a false tip that the Provos had robbed a jewelry store. When the police arrived, Van Duyn's girlfriend, Carla, was studying in Stolk's room. The police turned the place upside-down in their search for stolen diamonds, then escorted Carla and Auke Boersma to the police station. When police officers discovered Van Duyn in his apartment downstairs, they tried to force him to confess to the robbery, claiming that his girlfriend had already confessed. But he was able to prove that he had been at the theater on the evening of the robbery and the case was eventually dropped.

Support for the Provos varied within Amsterdam's government. Although members of non-religious parties on the city council were critical of the police actions, they basically agreed with Mayor Van Hall's opinions that the Provos shouldn't disturb public order, that automobile circulation took precedence over any Happenings, and that the Happenings shouldn't be allowed to continue. The Communists viewed the Provos as "petty-bourgeois, decadent half-baked intellectuals," but were concerned about the precedents set by the police that might undermine any future "genuine" Communist uprising. In August and September, two Communist members of the Amsterdam city council raised the question of police brutality. The police replied that they answered only to the national government in The Hague and not to the city council. Mayor Van Hall spoke out on behalf of law and order, citing a Dutch public opinion poll that showed that 81% of the population favored giving the Provos a spanking.

The Provos called the mayor's statements "insipid banalities." As far as they were concerned, the summer of 1965 had given shape to the Provo movement, which was growing from a handful of people with anarchist ideals into a movement with widespread political and cultural support.

In the weeks that followed, tension on the streets of Amsterdam mounted as every Happening became a confrontation with the authorities. With Van Hall's support, the police began to make arrests under Article 186 of the Criminal Law Code, which stated that when there is a mob, anyone who did not disperse in the event of a third order from the police would be considered to be participating in an illegal gathering and subject to imprisonment of up to three months or fines not to exceed 600 guilders (U.S. $200). Police surveillance of activity at the Lieverdje increased after the date of the Royal Wedding was set for March 10, 1966. The order to disperse under Article 186 became telegraphically short: "I request that you disperse. One, two, three, I have said it three times." Having given their three warnings, the police would arrest anyone present.

On October 7th, the Provos painted Mayor Van Hall's official residence on the Herengracht white. Thirty-four arrests were made on October 16th, and another 25 on October 23rd. On November 7th, the *Marechaussee* (Military Police) confiscated signs opposing the wedding at the historic but unoccupied Royal Palace on the Dam. By now the Marechaussee was guarding both the Palace and the National Monument on the Dam, as well as the Westerkerk, where the Royal Wedding was to take place. In his book, Van Duyn records the accelerating judicial penalties awarded against various Provos through the autumn season. On October 1st: fourteen days probation and a 25-guilder fine; on October 9th: three weeks in prison, of which two weeks were to be on probation; and on October 17th: six weeks imprisonment, of which four weeks were to be on probation. All this kept tension from lagging.

The Happenings at the Lieverdje continued into January 1966, but by the end of November 1965 attendance had dropped because of cold weather and because the police stopped making arrests. Provo riots had broken out across the country as local

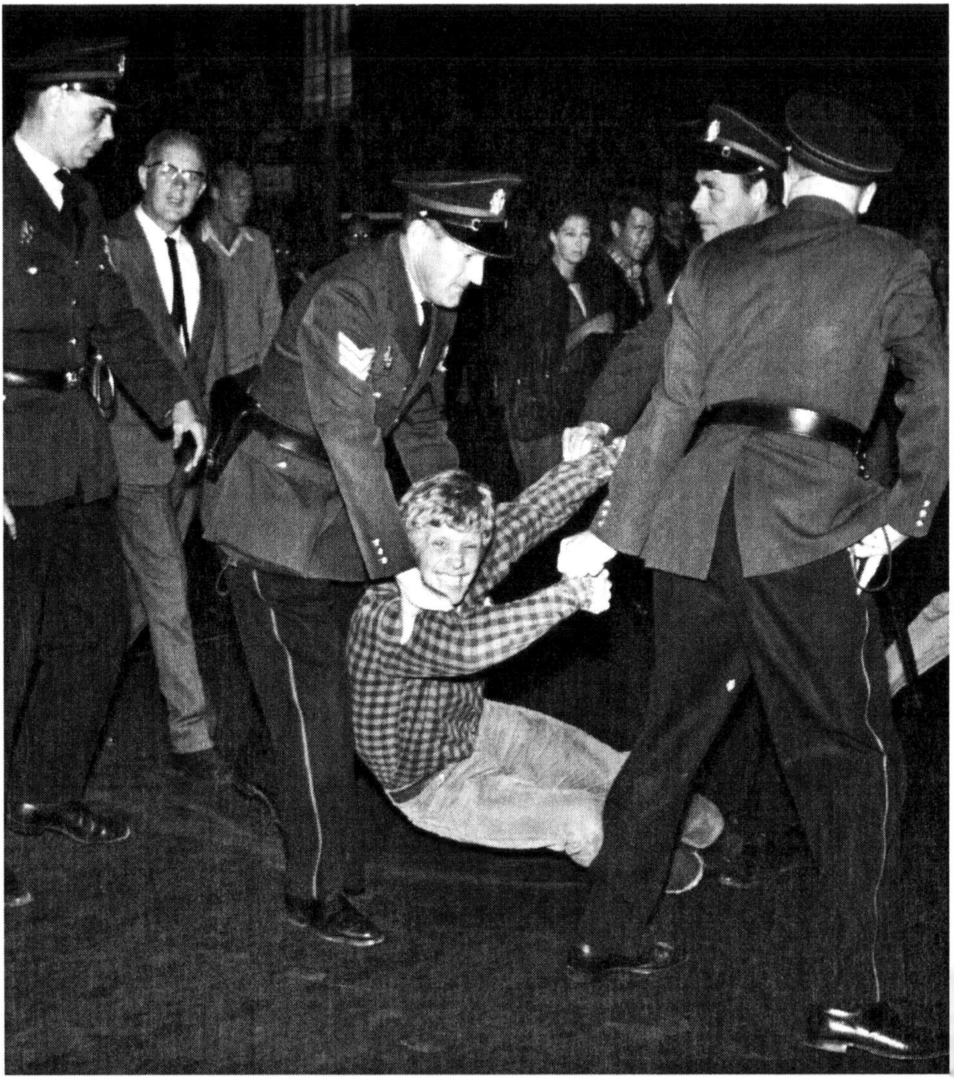

Rob Stolk carried off by the police.

youth besieged their own civic monuments. The fact that young people throughout the Netherlands were becoming anarchists alarmed the press. Among the cities swept by the "anarchist fad" were Barneveld, Bergen-op-Zoom, Heerlen, Venlo, Terneuzen, and Utrecht. The Utrecht *Stadsblad* called it the "Lieverdje sickness," and demanded that the police take care of the patient. But in Amsterdam itself, Provo was wrestling the monster of its own success. Van Duyn mentions the *Bastaard* group, which split from Provo in November 1965. He characterizes them as drug addicts (indicating just how strongly he himself rejected drugs) and notes that they lived together in the house of Joop Dielemans, who styled himself as "the anti-achievement painter." Bastaard criticized Provo for not being radical enough. The group promised to issue "an extremist, semi-literary, political pop-art magazine" so controversial that every issue would be confiscated. A pamphlet by Dielemans showed a policeman being choked by the hand of a Bastaard, but Van Duyn says that Bastaard's magazine never appeared because the group was too spaced-out to produce anything.

However, he does credit the Bastaard group with organizing the first anti-Vietnam War demonstration in the Netherlands, a sit-in at the entrance of the American Consulate in Amsterdam that took place on December 23rd, 1965. They invited the Provos and other groups to participate, and among the eventual protesters were Provo, the P.S.J.W. (Pacifist Socialist Youth Workgroups), the S.O.K. (Socialist Meeting Circles), and the S.J. (Socialist Youth of the Netherlands). This was the first of a series of demonstrations opposed to the Vietnam War and it also saw the first use of the Provo smoke bombs that were to figure so prominently at the Royal Wedding.

At that first demonstration Peter Bronkhorst set fire to an American flag and fled with police horsemen in hot pursuit as he ran down the busy Van Baerlestraat, where the old Amsterdam Concertgebouw is located. The chase went right through the heavy morning rush-hour traffic, which no doubt created a stirring image. The police then forced the demonstrators to leave the Consulate, so they headed across town to break a few windows at the American Express office.

In January 1966, the "*Provo-Oranje Committee, De Parel van de Jordaan*" (The Pearl of the Jordaan) was created. "The Pearl of the Jordaan," another name for the Provos, was to play an important role in the next few months. The Jordaan was the classic bohemian working-class quarter of Amsterdam, where Van Duyn, Stolk, and Grootveld all lived. In mid-January a bakfiets full of Provos dressed in orange with their faces painted the same color distributed leaflets against the monarchy. One featured a picture of Princess Bea-

10 maart
dag van de
anarchie

Provo flyer for the Day of Anarchy

trix on a new coin depicted as a Nazi collaborator punished by her neighbors after the Allied liberation by having her head shaved. The group, which included Rob Stolk and Hans Tuynman, was arrested at the Lieverdje.

Private local groups throughout the Netherlands had set up

a structure similar to the Community Chest in the United States to collect money for a "National Gift" from the Dutch people to the royal couple. The amount collected proved disappointing. In response, the Provo Oranje-Committee decided to launch an anti-gift campaign and issued a manifesto calling for a series of anti-fireworks and anti-festivities. The Anti-Wedding Gift campaign netted 500 guilders, with which the Provos purchased chemicals for the smoke bombs that they planned to launch along the route of the wedding procession on March 10th.

On the streets, the tension continued to mount. The Amsterdam police made a house-to-house search in the area of the Westerkerk after the sensationalist Belgian magazine *Kwik (Quicksilver)* reported that the Oranje-Committee had a hidden cannon aimed at the Westerkerk with the intention of splattering the official entourage with orange paint. Dutch newspapers carried a number of fantastic stories, including one that the Provos intended to blow on supersonic whistles to frighten the horses drawing the royal carriage, and another that the Provos planned to broadcast tapes of machine-gun fire in order to sow confusion among the police. A new White Plan, the White Explosion Plan, threatened to dump LSD into Amsterdam's drinking water, as a result of which the Marechaussee took up guard positions on the water system. The water was tested on a regular basis and the Tweede Kamer took only seven days to pass a bill outlawing LSD, a Dutch record for legislative action on any bill.

The police were in a panic. Ton Regtien, a Communist student leader who was quite critical of Provo, returned home a few days before March 10th to find the door to his room open and the floor littered with letters and newspaper clippings that he had been collecting. At first he thought that a neighbor had gone berserk, but later he read that a member of the city council had lodged a complaint against police raids and house searches similar to the one that he had experienced. The increasingly desperate police publicly justified their actions by claiming that they were searching for weapons. And on March 10th, 1966, the day of the Royal Wedding, the tension finally broke.

works referenced

Duyn (1967); Meier (1966); Mulisch (1967); Regtien (1967); Stansill and Mairowitz (1998); "The White Bicycle Plan" in *Delta* (1967).

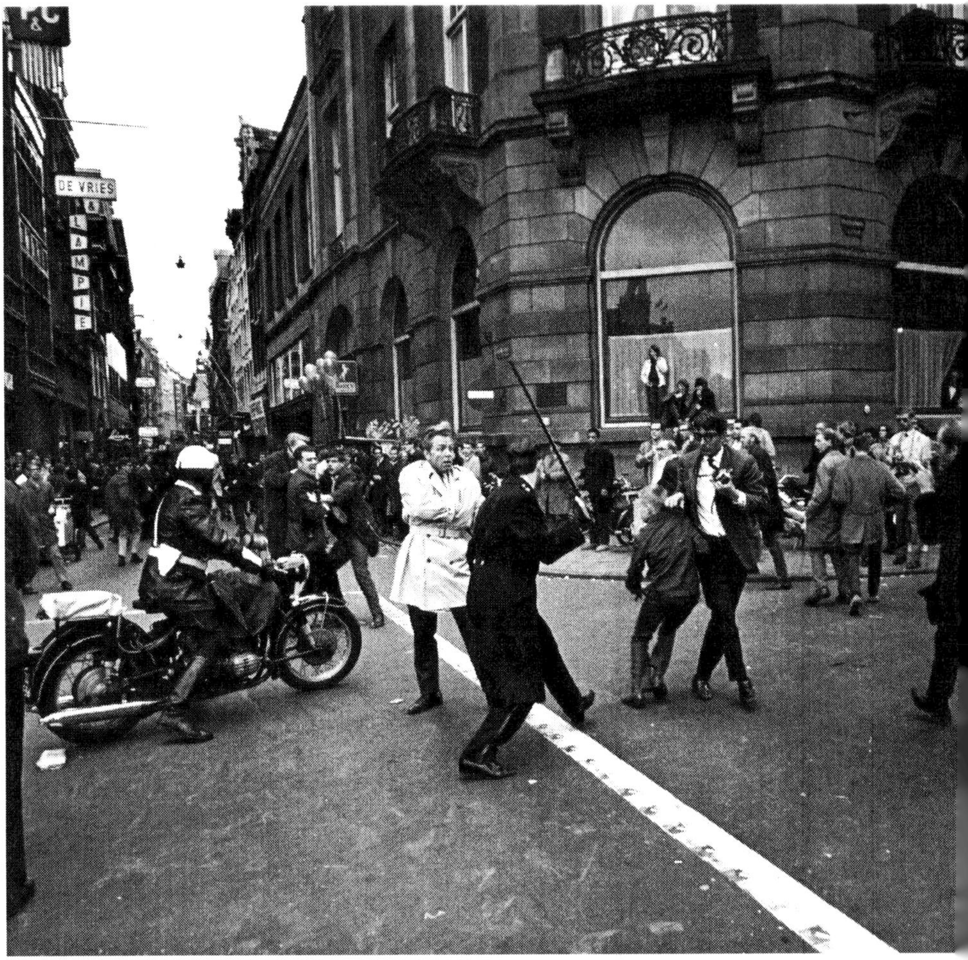

Amsterdam police attacking bystanders.

5. the finest hour of the dutch republic (march 10, 1966)

While it was impossible to predict what would happen during the March 10th wedding protests, both the Provos and the police had clear ideas of what they wanted to see. On March 9th it seemed as though the Government might have its way and the monolithic combination of press and government would hold an orderly ceremonial event, one greeted joyously by crowds of loyal Dutch citizens. By as early as March 5th, police raids had become a daily occurrence and much of Provo's literature was being confiscated. Many of the Provos were in hiding. Rob Stolk left the city for Zaandam and Grootveld spent his days at home, leaving his apartment only at night. Luud Schimmelpennick, the originator of the White Bicycle Plan, and Roel van Duyn hid out at the homes of friends. For the first time in months, the Lieverdje was quiet.

On February 25th, 1966, Van Duyn had published an article in *Provo* calling on the Amsterdam PROVOtariat to protest the wedding, saying that the traditional Proletariat could no longer be counted on because of the middle-class outlook ("embourgeoisement") exemplified by the Dutch Communist Party. Though the Marxists condemned this denigration of the Proletariat, the Provos had a very clear notion of their constituency.

WHAT IS THE PROVOTARIAT?

What is the PROVOtariat? Provos, beatniks, pleiners, nozems, teddy-boys, rockers, blousons noirs, hooligans, mangupi, students, artists, misfits, anarchists, ban-the-bombers.... Those who don't want a career and who lead irregular lives; those who come from the asphalt jungles of london, paris, amsterdam, new york, moscow, tokyo, berlin, milan, warsaw and who feel ill-adapted to this society.... The PROVOtariat is the last element of rebellion in our "developed" countries. The Proletariat is the slave of the politicians. Watching TV. It has joined its old enemy, the bourgeoisie, and now constitutes with the bourgeoisie a huge grey mass. The new class opposition in our countries is the PROVOtariat against this mass.

But the PROVOtariat is not a class — its make-up is too heterogeneous for that.

ANARCHY DEMANDS REVOLUTION

PROVO despairs of the coming Revolution and Anarchy. Nevertheless, it puts its faith in anarchism; for PROVO anarchism is the only admissible social concept. It is PROVO's ideological weapon against the authoritarian forces which oppose us.

If the PROVOtariat (so far) lacks the strength for revolution there is still — PROVOcation.

PROVOcation — with all its little pin pricks — has, in the face of circumstances, become our only weapon. It is our last chance to smash the authorities in their vital, soft parts. By our acts of provocation we force authority to tear off its mask. Uniforms, boots, kepis, swords, truncheons, fire hoses, police dogs, tear gas and all the other means of repression the authorities hold in reserve they must be forced to use against us. They will thus be forced to show their real nature; chin forward, eye-brows wrinkled, eyes glazed with rage, threatening left and right, commanding, forbidding, convicting.

They will make themselves more and more unpopular and the popular conscience will ripen for anarchy. THE CRISIS WILL COME. It is our last chance. A PROVOKED CRISIS FOR THE AUTHORITIES.

Such is the enormous provocation called for from the International PROVOtariat by PROVO — Amsterdam.

PROVOKE!!!
FORM ANARCHIST GROUPS!!!!
BEWARE! PROVOS, WE ARE LOSING A WORLD!!

(From *BAMN*, translation used with permission.)

The *Oranje-Comite* (Orange Committee) — *De Parel van de Jordaan* (The Pearl of the Jordaan) — called upon "The Monster of Amsterdam," the revolutionary Provotariat, to meet at the Dokwerker Monument at 9:30 A.M. on March 10th for a protest Happening. They chose the Dokwerker Monument for its symbolic importance as the site of the most significant workers' protest against anti-Semitic regulations in 1941 under the Nazi regime. The Dokwerker Monument stood at what had been the heart of the Jewish ghetto. It was yet another comment on Claus's Nazi past. In his account of the day's events, Van Duyn says that the Provos were hoping for a spontaneous massive protest, which turned out to be the case. To put it mildly, their expectations were exceeded.

Van Duyn's interesting account of the events surrounding March 10th complements Harry Mulisch's *Report to the King of Rats*, Hans Tuynman's *Full-Time Provo*, and an underappreciated book entitled *Provo: een jaar Provo activiteiten (Provo: a Year of Provo Activity)* by a journalist named De Jongh to fill out the record comprehensively. Planning for the demonstrations against the marriage inspired the first contact between the Provo movement and student opposition to the Establishment. *Propria Cures* (Latin for

"Mind your own business") was the student newspaper of the University of Amsterdam. Though its editors expressed opposition to the forthcoming marriage, when Grootveld called on them to ask if they were ready to work actively for the revolution they replied that they felt more comfortable behind their typewriters. By February 5th they had published an enthusiastic article on the Provos. They then joined with the Provos to bring out an "Orange Issue" of *Propria Cures* on March 5th. The Orange Issue included the same article, "The Practical Anarchist," that had resulted in *Provo #1* being confiscated in the summer of 1965. Though it was not confiscated, the Orange Issue marked the beginning of an uneasy alliance between the students and the Provos, one that eventually prompted Bernhard De Vries, a student activist, to join the Provos. (In June of 1966, De Vries would become the first successful Provo candidate for the Amsterdam City Council.)

As March 10th drew closer, the police continued to pressure people suspected of planning protests. On March 9th, Van Duyn returned home and only narrowly escaped a police raid on his apartment by slipping out a window and running up the fire escape to hide with neighbors. Other Provos were hiding at Hans Tuynman's apartment. They were all concerned about their safety as protestors, since a crowd that they estimated at a million pro-Orange (pro-monarchist) Dutchmen would be on hand for the wedding and might attack them as they demonstrated.

During the excitement of Van Duyn's escape, *Provo #7* came off the press as the first offset printing of the journal. Rob Stolk was upset with an article by Simon Vinkenoog, who was an advocate of psychedelic drugs. Stolk was concerned that Vinkenoog's article would tag the Provos as drug users. Tuynman argued the point with him. When an uneasy Van Duyn arrived at the apartment, a German journalist asked him about the actions planned for the next day.

While the group had various direct actions planned, the plan to use smoke bombs was causing a rift. Bernhard De Vries had ordered the smoke bombs weeks earlier from a 17-year-old student named Harman De Bont from the provincial town of Ede (pronounced: Aid-ah). De Bont was too frightened to actually make the bombs, but he delivered the chemical ingredients — potassium chlorate, sulfuric acid, nitrate, and powdered sugar — to De Vries on March 9th. De Vries took the bomb makings to the St. Olafspoort student club, against the wishes of the club's directors who feared a police raid. The directors insisted that the bombs be put together elsewhere, so De Vries visited Tuynman's apartment to enlist help with the assemblage.

Tuynman writes that both he and Peter Bronkhorst had been living on french fries for five days and that he hadn't had any sleep for three nights. They had serious doubts about the effectiveness of the smoke bombs as a tool of protest and were concerned for their personal safety. Tuynman insisted that it was more important to get out the latest issue of *Provo*, using this excuse to avoid helping with the smoke bombs. Someone showed up with a bundle of *Provo* #7 and Tuynman and Bronkhorst went with him to a basement where others were busily collating copies of the paper. But Stolk and Van Duyn left with De Vries.

Fortunately for them, the Provos at Tuynman's learned in time that a neighbor had informed the police of their whereabouts, and each of them sped off with a bundle of *Provo* #7, leaving the neighbor screaming after them. They reconvened at the apartment of Duco Van Weerlee, another Provo. Several teenage Provos joined them there, having fled from the homes of their angry parents after the police had put them under house arrest. *Provo* #7 was ready for distribution by 1:00 A.M.

It was already March 10th. No one knew Van Duyn's whereabouts. His girlfriend, Carla, was so worried that she thought of telephoning the police, who could at least have confirmed his arrest, had that been the case. But the group decided against that move, and Tuynman left Van Weerlee's apartment at 3:00 A.M. to get some sleep.

While Tuynman slept, Martin Visser and Peter Bronkhorst concocted a batch of smoke bombs. Another batch was assembled during a party at the floating home of Kees Hoeker, proprietor of the Lowland Weed Company, a houseboat marijuana farm that became a famous alternative tourist attraction in the 1970s. (In addition to helping with the smoke bombs, Hoeker was preparing for the "White Chicken Happening" that he staged later in the day.) At 5:30 A.M., Peter Bronkhorst woke Tuynman. Bronkhorst had several smoke bombs with him, and he and Tuynman were able to reach the heavily patrolled Raadhuistraat, which was directly on the route of the wedding procession, only because the out-of-town police units in the area didn't recognize them.

De Jongh's *Provo: A Year of Provo Activity* reports that at 1:00 A.M. on the morning of March 10th he was at the bar of the Krasnapolsky Hotel on the Dam, Amsterdam's large central square. The hotel faces the vacant and ceremonial Royal Palace on the far side of the square and was press central for some 600 international correspondents assembled to cover the wedding. De Jongh was drinking with the many journalists. Outside, numerous policemen were patrolling Dam square. Already some monarchists had gathered to claim their places along the procession route, but earlier that evening smoke bombs had gone off at the Royal Palace, and the police, who were clearly on edge, had begun attacking innocent bystanders. At one point the entire square had been cleared, even of the monarchist *Oranjeklanten*.

The wedding procession was scheduled to begin at the Dam, proceeding eventually to the Raadhuisstraat, which led some seven blocks to the gold-domed Westerkerk (West Church) where the couple would be married. At 3:00 A.M., Harry Mulisch and several other writers joined De Jongh at the hotel. The new arrivals complained of the police brutality they had witnessed as they drove around the city, but had seen no signs of protest.

Police barriers had been set up along the entire procession route, and at 8:00 A.M. the center of Amsterdam was closed to automobile traffic. The police were spot-checking automobiles as they entered Amsterdam, patrolling the highways from The Hague, Amersfoort, and Utrecht. Nevertheless, sporadic protests continued to spread across the city.

When Bronkhorst and Tuynman arrived at Raadhuistraat they heard people yelling, "*Claus raus!*" and cries of "*Republiek, Republiek, Republiek!*" Young demonstrators had occupied the graceful Victorian galleries of the Raadhuistraat. As one regiment of soldiers marched by, demonstrators cried out mockingly, "*Ein-Zwei, Ein-Zwei!*" (German for "One-Two, One-Two"). On the opposite side of the street, the pro-monarchist Oranjeklanten applauded the troops.

At the Krasnapolsky Hotel, Mulisch watched the preparations for the procession on television and, like the majority of Netherlanders, thought hopelessly that all protest against the wedding had been contained. Suddenly, the television rang with people shouting, "*Oranje boven, Oranje boven, Leve de Republiek!*" (Up with Orange, Long Live the Republic!). Though the cameras swerved away from the ensuing violence, Mulisch noticed a white cloud, which he thought might possibly be a break in the transmission. But it wasn't! The haze on the television screen was something else! When Mulisch realized it was a smoke bomb and that a mass protest was beginning he was overcome with emotion. (Van Duyn says that some 200 smoke bombs were set off throughout the day. In all, 26 people were arrested.)

By 9:30 A.M., a crowd of several hundred had assembled for the protest at the Dokwerker Monument on the Meijerplein, a half-mile east of Dam Square across the Amstel River. The demonstrators moved out towards Raadhuistraat shortly after 9:30 A.M. As they crossed over the Amstel River, they could hear smoke bombs going off in the center of the city. The crowd managed to reach the procession route via the Blauwbrug, Reguliersbreestraat, the Munt, and Kalverstraat, in spite of the police guard. The Provo "army" moved out on the Spui, yelling, "Republiek! Republiek!" and singing "Oranje boven, Leve de Republiek." Then more police showed

Smoke bombs on the Dam.

up, some of them mounted on horseback, to disperse the protestors. The crowd was a milling mix of "Republican" youth, monarchist Oranjeklanten, and various police and military units. By the time they reached the Raadhuisstraat, Van Duyn estimates that as 5,000 protestors were there. The crowd was dispersed on the Raadhuisstraat by repeated police charges. One demonstrator was knocked unconscious. Few monarchists remained.

Van Duyn speaks of a completed process, what he calls the politicalization of the *provocerende nozempje* (the provocative "little" delinquent) who had now become a conscious revolutionary. The Provos had been highly doubtful about the public response to their call for a demonstration against the wedding on March 10th. They feared that a small response would be smothered in a sea of pro-Orange Netherlanders caught up in patriotic zeal for the Monarchy. The wave of 5,000 young demonstrators astounded them (and everyone else). The Provo call had touched off a frenzy of anti-authoritarianism directed against the Dutch bourgeois society of the day, which young Netherlanders felt as suffocating. The reaction to the call was spontaneous: the crowds of demonstrators filling the streets of Amsterdam that day were forming what Jean-Paul Sartre calls the "Fused Group," a spontaneous crowd that launches a revolution. (See Appendix 7)

At 10:30 A.M., an hour after the Dutch battleship "H.M.S. De Ruyter" gave a 21-cannon salute from Het IJ, Amsterdam's harbor, the royal guests were seated in their limousines on the Dam. Beatrix and Claus got into the Golden Coach and the procession moved towards the Raadhuis and old Stadhuis (the new and old City Halls), situated at the time on the charming and ancient Oude Zijds Voorburgwal canal, before heading for the Westerkerk. The protests there began almost immediately after Mayor Van Hall delivered a welcoming speech to the royal couple. Willem-Jan Stevens, a Provo who lived next door to the old Stadhuis, threw a rat from his window at the Golden Coach. He had also planned to blast tapes of Hitler's speeches out over the canal, but someone tipped off the police and they climbed to the roof and dismantled his equipment.

The wedding procession was finally moving towards the Westerkerk at 11:45 A.M., about the time that the Dutch Army and National Police units first charged into the crowd of almost 2,000 protestors streaming from the Dokwerker Monument. Initially, things were fairly quiet. A few smoke bombs greeted the wedding party in the Paleisstraat. But when it passed over the bridge on Raadhuisstraat spanning the Herrengracht canal, Kees Hoeker tossed a white chicken into the path of the Golden Coach, causing the horses to bolt. (An angry monarchist threw Hoeker into the canal, from which the Waterways Police rescued him.)

Meanwhile, swelling as it moved, the Dokwerker demonstration headed inexorably in the direction of the Westerkerk. The first skirmishes between police and demonstrators broke out in the Kalverstraat, a narrow pedestrian shopping street that runs from the Dam to Muntplein. It was at this point in time that Hans Tuynman and Peter Bronkhorst threw their smoke bombs at the wedding procession in the Raadhuisstraat. De Jongh writes that Bronkhorst threw the largest bomb, the one that enveloped the Golden Coach in white smoke for several minutes and became the image that appeared on the front pages of the world press.

The smoke bombs were wrapped in tinfoil. Tuynman describes how he tore one open with his thumbnail, lit it with a cigarette, and dropped it at his feet, trembling. He was immediately enveloped by a cloud of white smoke. Chaos erupted, with police running everywhere. Tuynman ran off, leaving the sound of battle behind him. He saw Peter Bronkhorst take flight. A policeman on horseback swung at him with a nightstick, missed, and Bronkhorst disappeared into the crowd. According to Bronkhorst, a young fellow came by on a bicycle, a complete stranger. Bronkhorst jumped on the back of the bicycle, whispered "Police," and the two of them sped off.

The police and the Marechaussee attacked from the Muntplein to drive the Dokwerker demonstrators out of the Kalverstraat, but only succeeded in pushing them closer to the Westerkerk. By now police activity was uncoordinated, though they did have orders not to let any more protestors onto the Raadhuisstraat in the area of the Westerkerk. There were already many injuries on both sides of the battle line. The few Provos who had already snuck through the cordon continued to set off smoke bombs and light orange flags afire. Another group of Provos succeeded in surprising the police by sailing down the Prinsengracht canal, landing near the Westerkerk.

Press coverage of the events shows the police and the Marechaussee repeatedly hammering into the demonstrators, mostly younger people, and beating them brutally. Television broadcasts show crowds of young people shouting "*Leve de Republiek*" as they flee the pursuing police. General public sympathy for the police changed during the day to sympathy for the demonstrators. By the time the wedding service in the Westerkerk was over, the protestors had been dispersed, but a tense atmosphere hung over the city.

Van Duyn notes a grave tactical error on the part of the police: they should have dispersed the crowd at the Dokwerker Monument and closed off the bridge over the Amstel River. The demonstrations put March 10th on the front page of the world press, and he asserts that in Amsterdam itself enthusiasm for the Provos reached new heights. "New faces, both insane and intelligent, adhered to the cause." The first printing of *Provo* #7, 3,000 copies, sold out in three days.

The conservative press, however, strove to minimize the international impact of the coverage. It reported Chief Inspector Heyink of the Amsterdam police saying that all went well, except for some minor incidents. In *De Telegraaf*, an infamous journalist named Jacques Gans (a Dutch Westbrook Pegler) tried to smear the Provos by comparing them to the Nazi Brownshirts and characterizing the demonstrators as several hundred youths entirely unaware of the fact that they were demonstrating against the marriage. An editorial from the shocked *Elsevier's Weekblad*, a Dutch weekly magazine as stodgy as the old *Time* or *Newsweek*, insisted that the Provo leaders had somehow lured several thousand young people into the streets while they themselves kept out of sight. The editorial argued that there was absolutely no justification for the demonstrations.

Premier Cals, who must ultimately bear responsibility for what happened, blamed the demonstrations on the foreign press, whom he charged with subsidizing the protests. Van Duyn considers Cals to be the big loser of March 10th, saying that it was his hope for dominance over public dissent that led to the events of the day. Shortly after March 10th, the De Parel van de Jordaan Committee credited Mayor Van Hall with puncturing the image of a popularly supported marriage by virtue of the police violence that he unleashed. They considered the events to be of "pop art dimension" and told the mayor that they hoped to make use of more of his brilliant ideas in the future. (In actual fact, Van Hall had opposed holding the wedding in Amsterdam but was overruled by Premier Cals, who had persisted in adhering to Princess Beatrix's wishes, stubbornly refusing to reverse his decision in an attempt to maintain government prestige.)

The Regent mentality and a generally officious insensitivity toward the citizens of Amsterdam had combined to create a situation that was beyond official control. The incident at the Anne Frank House, which is located on the Prinsengracht Canal, next to the Westerkerk, exemplifies just how obtuse the bureaucrats had become. The house is run by an international student organization that conducts tours through the secret apartment where the Frank family hid from the Nazis. In her famous diary, Anne writes about looking out from her hiding place at the church tower and listening to the peal of its bells. Yet, despite their knowledge of Claus's Nazi past, the Amsterdam police vainly requested the use of the house as its headquarters for the duration of the wedding ceremonies. In view of the popular grounds for opposition to the marriage, their enormous lack of tact hardly merits comment.

In their exuberance, the Provos had spawned a number of wild ideas for direct actions, which they never managed to execute. They envisaged filling the organ of the Westerkerk with laughing gas; they contemplated collecting lion shit from the Amsterdam Zoo and spreading it along the procession route in hopes of frightening the horses in the procession; and, as mentioned in the previous chapter, they fantasized about spiking Amsterdam's drinking water with LSD. Nevertheless, what passed on March 10th was the finest hour of the first Dutch Republic. The events of that day set the scene for struggles that would unfold during the following three months, climaxing on June 14th 1966 in the full-fledged Battle of Amsterdam. The tide had turned. From beneath Amsterdam's placid surface, an anarchist rebellion was rising to take form.

works referenced

De Jongh (1966); Duyn (1967); Mulisch (1967); Stansill and Mairowitz (1998); Tuynman (1967).

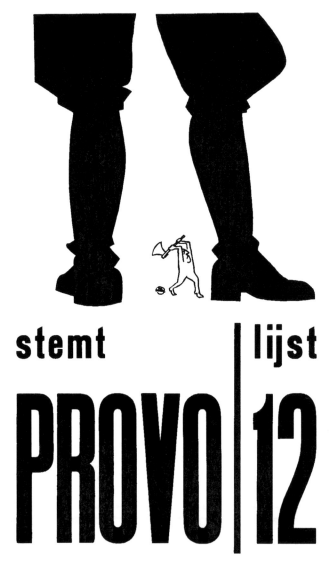

Provo election poster

6. the two dimensions of police brutality: amsterdam under seige (june 15, 1966–may 14, 1967)

In the aftermath of March 10th, several student groups organized a photography exhibit on police brutality. They chose to hang it at the gallery of Polak & Van Gennep, a socialist publishing house located at 820 Prinsengracht not far from the Amstelveld and the Rembrandtplein, with the opening scheduled for Saturday, March 19th. On the day of the opening an ironic twist was introduced when the Amsterdam Police staged a brutal "opening Happening," replicating the content of the exhibition photographs on the street outside the gallery. Roel Van Duyn acknowledged the rich surrealist irony of the opening when he called the event a *spiegelbeeld-provokatie* (mirror image provocation), highlighting the fact that spectators were viewing photographs of previous police violence inside the gallery at the same time as they witnessed continuing violence live on the street outside.

Dutch novelist Jan Wolkers had planned to open the exhibition with a symbolic repeat of Kees Hoeker's March 10th White Chicken Happening, when he threw a chicken into the path of the royal coach. By now, white chickens had become the Provo symbol for the police. Auke Boersma had brought twenty of them to the gallery expecting to present one to Wolkers. Boersma and Wolkers intended to release it with a note to the Vietnamese people. Once the chicken reached Vietnam, they claimed, there would be peace. But the student organizers refused to let Boersma bring the bird into the gallery. Instead, someone outside (presumably Boersma) lobbed the chicken over the heads of the people lined up to enter the exhibit and, leaning out a window, Jan Wolkers caught it. With that, the exhibition "opened."

Unfortunately, a neighbor with no sense of humor had phoned the police. When a patrol car arrived there was a scuffle and ten of Boersma's chickens were "arrested" by the two patrol officers. During the incident, one of the officers hit a girl in the face. Refusing to be intimidated by the violence, the other visitors lined up outside continued waiting to enter the gallery. So the patrolmen called their station for reinforcements. Twenty-six more police officers soon appeared, wading in with clubs to disperse the crowd because they claimed it was blocking the little bit of Saturday-afternoon traffic passing by. A new Provo White Chicken Plan called for the evolution of the police from "Blue Chickens" (the color of their uniforms) to "White Chickens," friendly non-violent white-clad social workers of the future. The entire text was an elaborate pun on the Dutch word *kip* (chicken), which had become street slang for policeman. When Boersma attempted to defuse the situation by presenting a copy of the Plan to the police attacking the crowd he was clubbed in the face for his trouble. Numerous photographers, and filmmaker Louis Van Gasteren, all on hand to view the exhibit, alertly recorded these new incidents of police brutality. (By the end of the incident, two people had been hospitalized with brain concussions.)

POLICE — A BETTER IMAGE
MARCH 10: A BAD OMEN

This warning by the Orange Committee, The Pearl of the Jordaan has alas become a hard truth. The slaughter on March 10 led directly to the founding of "The Society of Friends of the Police," whose aim is to re-establish the image of the policeman as your best friend. The white chicken with the white cap is an anarchist. Henri Knap has been invited to launch the "white cap action." Honorary membership on our white list has been offered to Jan Wolkers, the notorious Mayor of Amsterdam G.V. Hall, and the man with the chicken. They will receive the white chicken badge.

The WHITE CHICKEN PLAN

Ask the White Chicken for Chicken.

The Society of Friends of the Police puts forward the following programme: The blue chicken becomes a white chicken. This is demonstrated by the wearing of white uniforms. The SFP agrees to a transitional period during which blue caps are exchanged for white ones. The white chicken will use the white bicycle. Outside the Magic Center's canal area the so-called police cars can be used as "tinned chicken." The white chicken is unarmed and instead will carry a bag containing medicine, aspirin, matches, [and] little orange slices with chicken meat.

The French King Henri IV formulated the materialistic ideal as: "A chicken in the pot every day." White chicken is the cheapest kind of meat with the necessary animal protein. It will be issued by the municipality and distributed by Amsterdam's social workers among the suffering population.

WHY NOT HAVE FUN CHICKEN IS IN CHICKEN IS FUN

CHICKEN IS GOOD FOR YOU

Harry Mulisch arrived at the gallery, but was unable to get in, due to the overflowing crowd. Instead he went to the Sint Olofspoort student club, one canal away, on the Keizersgracht, to view a private

The Provo Witte Kippen Plan (White Chicken Plan) and Witte Fiets Plan (White Bicycle Plan). "Kip" (chicken) is slang for police. The plan was for reform of the Amsterdam Police, converting them to social workers. The White Bicycle was for the city to put thousands of free bicycles at the disposal of the population in order to solve automobile congestion in the city. The man to the left of the front wheel of the bicycle, with the cigarette in his mouth is probably Peter Bronkhorst. This event took place on March 19th on the Prinsengracht at the photo exhibition of police brutality at the royal wedding on March 10th, occasioning in turn another round of police brutality.

screening of a film documenting the March 10th police brutality. The audience at Sint Olofspoort couldn't understand why the soundtrack was only playing the sirens and not the voices of people in the film. It wasn't until they left the club that they realized that the "problem" with the soundtrack was that it was being drowned out by the "mirroring" commotion outside. March 10th was being repeated.

Nico Scheepmaker, a journalist for the politico-literary monthly *Hollands Maandblad*, also witnessed some of the events of

March 19th. He was on the Prinsengracht when he ran into his friend and colleague Joop Van Tijn, who was walking with his wife. Then the three of them met Jan Wolkers and his wife. By then, Wolkers had left the gallery and was walking down the Prinsengracht with the white chicken tucked under his arm. As the five of them left the Prinsengracht a police Volkswagen pulled up and Wolkers was accused of leading a demonstration.

Scheepmaker parted company with the Wolkers' and went to view the Sint Olofspoort film, where he heard about the attack on the people at the Polak & Van Gennep gallery. Wary of encountering the police, he went to the gallery but kept to the opposite side of the canal and entered a café containing several other journalists. The owner locked up, and he and his patrons watched the police violence through the windows of the café.

Harry Mulisch and some of the more prominent Provos passed the café window. Soon afterward more police cars and a paddy wagon arrived bringing a new shipment of clubs to the police. Within an hour things had quieted down and the police had left. But when Scheepmaker left the café to get his car he saw a group including Mulisch and journalist Braam De Swaan staring in astonishment at a row of mounted police just off the Rembrandtplein. The police seemed ready to charge if needed as reinforcements. De Swaan squatted to see if all the horses were in line and even gave sardonically helpful advice: "Fifth horse, a bit forward."

The events of that afternoon were followed by what Mulisch calls the "Provo Night of March 19th." That night ten thousand Catholics from all over the Netherlands were scheduled to hold the annual *Stille Omgang* (Silent Procession) in the center of the city. The Stille Omgang honored the "Miracle of Amsterdam" of 1345, when a consecrated wafer was given in absolution to a dying man, who vomited it up. The man survived, and the wafer, though tossed with the vomit into a fire that was kept blazing throughout the night, was discovered among the glowing embers the next day to be unburned, quite cool, and pure white. The procession had been prohibited during the Protestant Reformation and only permitted to resume in 1881. The route wound down older side streets that had once been the main streets of Medieval Amsterdam, including the Warmoesstraat and the Nes, then crossed over to the Kalverstraat and returned to the Nieuwedijk. At its southernmost extreme, the procession route passed within a block of the Lieverdje, on the Spui, where the Provos were planning to hold a Happening to protest the police action earlier in the day.

Mayor Van Hall instructed Police Commissioner Landman to restrain all police activity, except patrols required to intervene in actual criminal acts. Catholics and Protestants formed two major pillars of the Zuilen System, the structure upon which political power rested in the Netherlands. Van Hall did not want to see a Catholic procession that had been reinstituted after a 300-year ban transformed into a riot in the Protestant official capital of a Protestant country in which Catholics constitute a major voting block. He worried that another Provo "riot Happening" might spill over into the route of the Stille Omgang at the point where it turned into the Kalverstraat, disrupting the procession.

The police assigned to watch the Provos, many of whom were in plain clothes, waited out the Provo Happening at the Lieverdje. As Van Hall recalls it, when the Provos failed to provoke the police they headed for the monumental (and unoccupied) Royal Palace on the Dam to set fires in the porticos of the building. Commissioner Landman immediately dispatched his Mobile Unit to the scene of the fires, but the Provo demonstrators were gone by the time it arrived. They continued their night of demonstrations by gathering outside the Mayor's official residence on Van Beethovenstraat to shout their disapproval at him. Then, according to Hans Tuynman, they moved on to the Van Heutz Monument.

That evening, VARA (*Verenigde Arbeiders* Radio Amateurs), the radio/television network connected to the Dutch Socialist Party, broadcast Louis Van Gasteren's footage of the police violence outside the Polak & Van Gennep gallery. That was followed by a televised speech by Mayor Van Hall, who called on people to understand the young people of the day and asked for an *Afkoelingsperiode* ("a cooling off period," borrowed from American Sixties journalese). In his speech, Van Hall mentioned a Jewish policeman whom protestors had heckled as a Nazi SS officer. (In his book, Van Duyn notes dryly that the officer was behaving like a Nazi at the time.)

Despite Van Hall's call for calm, his speech put an obvious agenda in play. The Mayor was hoping to demonize the Provos for targeting a Jew. The anecdote about the heckling was a strategic appeal to the strong pro-Jewish sentiment of Amsterdam. But a series of events followed that the Mayor could not have predicted. First, the popular Dutch television equivalent of *That Was the Week That Was (Zo Dan Nog Eens Een Keer)*, presented a skit satirizing Van Hall. In it an actor parodied a Van Hall interview, repeating the phrase "Jewish policeman" until he becomes hypnotized by it. Incessantly screaming "Jewish cop," the Mayor is eventually straightjacketed and led away by two hospital attendants. The skit upset the Socialist Party because it insulted Van Hall, a party member. And since VARA was connected to the Socialist Party, it refused to broadcast the program until the skit was cut. The cast refused to comply, and the liveliest Dutch television show of the day fell victim to censorship imposed by the Dutch Socialist Party.

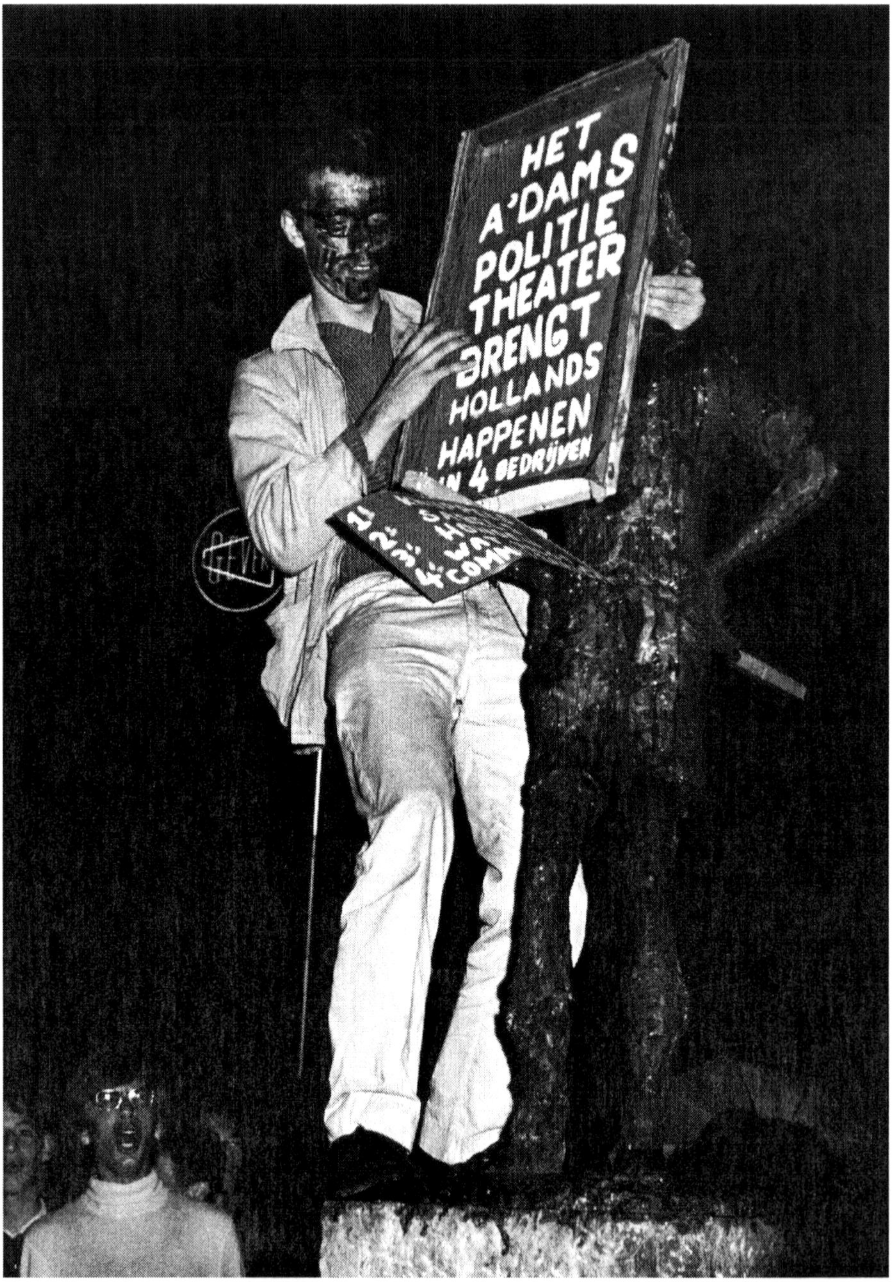

Provo Luud Schimmelpenninck on the Lieverdje statue. His sign reads, "The Amsterdam Police Theater presents Holland Happenings in Four Acts."

Another unforeseen consequence of Van Hall's VARA speech came when Robert Jasper Grootveld reacted to it. Grootveld identified with the plight of the Jewish policeman, and saw the insult from the Provo side as a sign that the level of violence had become intolerable. He felt personally responsible for what was occurring, and decided to withdraw from Provo activity, and indeed from Amsterdam and the Netherlands. He chose instead to pass the next five months on an extended vacation in the Mediterranean, not returning to Amsterdam until September.

It is striking to realize that, while Grootveld was indispensable in sparking the initial momentum toward Provo's emergence, his absence did not hinder the movement's onward development. In fact, the period following his withdrawal came to be seen as the peak of Provo's two-year lifespan. And by the time he returned in September, even Grootveld's formidable creativity and charisma could not save Provo from the decline that led to its eventual demise.

One unexpected attack on the Provos came from one of the two Socialist newspapers. An editorial in *Het Vrije Volk (The Free People)* declared that the police had the right to use force against demonstrations that protested police brutality. The editors of the paper called for sentences of several months' imprisonment without parole for any arrested demonstrators. They claimed that such severe measures would contribute to the cooling-off period. "Street terror, from whatever side, is unacceptable in the Netherlands," the editorial paradoxically concluded, clearly favoring the police.

On March 21st, a coalition of student groups, Young Socialists, Provos, and Communists formed the *Komite 19.3.66* (March 19th 1966 Committee). Hans Tuynman, who attended the six-hour opening meeting, expressed skepticism about Provo's connection with the Committee, worrying about the danger that such a broad coalition posed for the richly surrealistic Provo imagination. At that first meeting, the coalition rejected the White Chicken Plan, dismissed the Happenings as "apolitical," and rejected a proposed teach-in with the Amsterdam police. The only item approved was a motion to file a complaint with the national Ministry of Interior about the police violence at the photography exhibit on March 19th.

According to Van Duyn, the Committee should have been called the March 10th Movement, and should not have emphasized cooling-off, but rather have actively sought a solution to ongoing problems. He describes the coalition as a New Left front, but noted that the two Communist student groups, the ANJV and the OPSJ, operated in the sphere of the Old Left. Most Communist youth belonged to the ANJV and the OPSJ because their parents were long-time members of the Dutch Communist Party. Their spokesman was Roel Walraven, a 36-year-old member of the Amsterdam city council. Van Duyn does, nevertheless, praise the Socialist Youth in the coalition for their willingness to participate in "illegal demonstrations." The Provos viewed the term "illegal demonstrations" as a built-in contradiction. They were adamantly opposed to asking permission to hold demonstrations, because for them freedom included the right to demonstrate. They felt that their only responsibility lay in announcing their demonstrations in order to better enable the police to regulate traffic.

However, so as not to antagonize the coalition and in concert with the Committee, the Provos sought permission for a demonstration scheduled for March 26th. They asked to protest against police violence in Amsterdam and they made the following demands:

1. That both the mayor and the police chief be removed from office;
2. That the police be made answerable to charges of brutal ity to the City Council;
3. For a general reorganization of the Police Department;
4. That the Mayor of Amsterdam be elected rather than appointed.

(It's interesting to note here that the first demand was actually realized in 1967, as was the third, to a degree — the police now answer to a triumvirate: the Mayor, the Chief Officer of Justice, and the Police Commissioner. However, Dutch mayors are still appointed by the Crown, the Queen and her ministers select the citizen they consider an appropriate designate. Mayor Van Hall, for example, had been a war hero who served as the treasurer of the Dutch resistance movement, and was a member of the Socialist Party, the majority party in Amsterdam.)

On March 26, five members of the coalition met with Van Hall. Tuynman was originally delegated as the Provo representative, but he couldn't make it in time and Van Duyn attended instead. Van Hall attempted to reassure the group, telling them that a nephew of his wore a beard, a sign at that time of social rebellion. That was the extent of his sympathy. He denied permission for the demonstration because of threats against the Provos that he claimed to have received by letter and telephone. He also expressed doubt about the coalition's ability to control its membership, despite a monitoring corps that had been organized for that specific purpose. (The March 19th 1966 Committee had rejected a Provo proposal to identify monitors with a "third eye" painted on their foreheads, but the existence of the corps negated the Mayor's reasoning.)

Rather than openly defy Van Hall, the Provos organized a "demonstration of the spontaneous organization and solidarity of the provotariat." As *Provokatie #12*, Duco Van Weerlee and Van

Duyn produced the "Manifesto to the Amsterdam Provotariat," calling for a general absence Happening and temporary coexistence with the *klootjesvolk* (a tern the Provos were now employing to mean "the common run of people"). That Saturday they held their "absence Happening" at the Lieverdje. Hardly anyone came to the Spui that evening, and the Provos claimed victory over Van Hall by virtue of the fact that by clearing the Spui of demonstrators they achieved something that the police and government could no longer accomplish.

Provokatie #12 resulted in another meeting with Van Hall, which took place the following Thursday. The Mayor objected to anti-police language in the manifesto, and, more personally, to the fact that two roast chickens had been delivered to his home. By then the chicken had become a derogatory synonym for the police in much the way that "pig" came to be used in the United States. The Mayor said that he would only permit a demonstration as long as signs reading, "Van Hall met vakantie" (Vacation for Van Hall) and "Van der Molen weg" (Down with Van der Molen) were not displayed. He claimed that demonstrations against specific persons were unlawful. The Committee refused to accept his terms. Instead they forced him to tip his hand by requesting permission for a demonstration on April 4th that would feature only slogans like "Democracy," "Freedom of Expression," and "Right to Demonstrate." Van Hall refused to permit it. But this time, the coalition planned to protest anyway, on Saturday, April 2nd.

The April 2nd action was called an "individual demonstration" to avoid the implication of full-scale defiance. On April 1st, Hans Tuynman was passing out leaflets calling for participation in the individual demonstration. When he passed a leaflet to two policemen as an April Fools' joke, he was arrested for inciting sedition. He was detained for five days at the Marnixstraat police station, then sent to the *Huis van Bewaring* (House of Detention) prison on the Amstelveense Weg on April 6th. He was freed on April 15th on the condition that he not participate in any activity or assembly that might disturb public order. (An impossibility for a Provo!) In the interim, the April 2nd "individual" demonstration had gone ahead without permission, without signs or slogans, and without interference from the police.

On April 23rd it was ruled that Tuynman violated his parole by disturbing the peace when he shouted "Imaazje" during an event at the Lieverdje. He was returned to the Huis van Bewaring prison. On April 27th the prosecutor asked for a three-month sentence, one month of which would be probation, but the judge decided on a full three-month term. Tuynman appealed, winning his release two weeks short of his full sentence.

Van Duyn considered the repeated arrests and successive sentences a new strategy on the part of the authorities. The judiciary was clearly aiming its energies against the Provo movement fully as much as the police were. In Mulisch's analysis, this was due to the paternalistic outlook of the judiciary, which he found guilty of caste justice, where citizens were unequal before their judges. The attitude manifested in various ways. One judge, named Stheeman, told a Provo: "You can't pass judgment on the War because you didn't take part in it." As Mulisch points out, such an outlook puts an end to history, as well as to the need for a judiciary.

The judicial assault was random but persistent. On April 2nd the editors of the Sint Olafspoort club student newspaper, *Bikkelklacht*, had been detained for four days for offending Princess Beatrix solely because their most recent cover featured a girl in a bathing suit who bore a striking resemblance to her. That same day an 18-year-old boy was arrested on the Spui simply for yelling "fascist" at police officers. He was sentenced to eight weeks of prison, five of which he would be on probation.

Both the judicial and legislative branches of government seemed to believe that the only way to regain their prestige and authority lay in revoking civil liberties, above all freedom of speech. In the *Eerste Kamer* (Upper Chamber of Parliament), a member of the KVP (Catholic People's Party) named Van Lieshout took exception to an anonymous absurd parody in *Provo* #7 that facetiously called for blowing up the IJ Tunnel and liquidating the tunnel's architect, De Gier. The tunnel was intended to pass under Amsterdam's huge harbor and connect the northern quarter of the city with the center. When asked his opinion of the article, De Gier read it with amusement and said that he did not feel at all threatened. Yet on April 4th, Prosecutor J. H. Hartsuiker ordered the arrest of Van Duyn, Schimmelpennick, Rob Stolk, and Hans Metz, who were held to be responsible for the article. The basis of the case lay in Hartsuiker's contention that, while stable intellectuals might find the article amusing, it could inspire some readers to commit acts of violence. The Prosecutor insisted that the court had to consider insane or paranoid people, which led the defense to reply: "Then we must ban all films, books, and newspapers." Each of the defendants was jailed and charged with inciting seditious acts. On May 27th the assistant prosecutor, Renesse, asked the court for a three-month sentence for Van Duyn (of which one month would be on probation); ten weeks for Stolk (of which six weeks would be probation), and lesser sentences for the other two defendants. Ultimately, Van Duyn was sentenced to six weeks, Stolk to four weeks, and Schimmelpennick to three weeks.

And while these cases were in process, the judicial assault

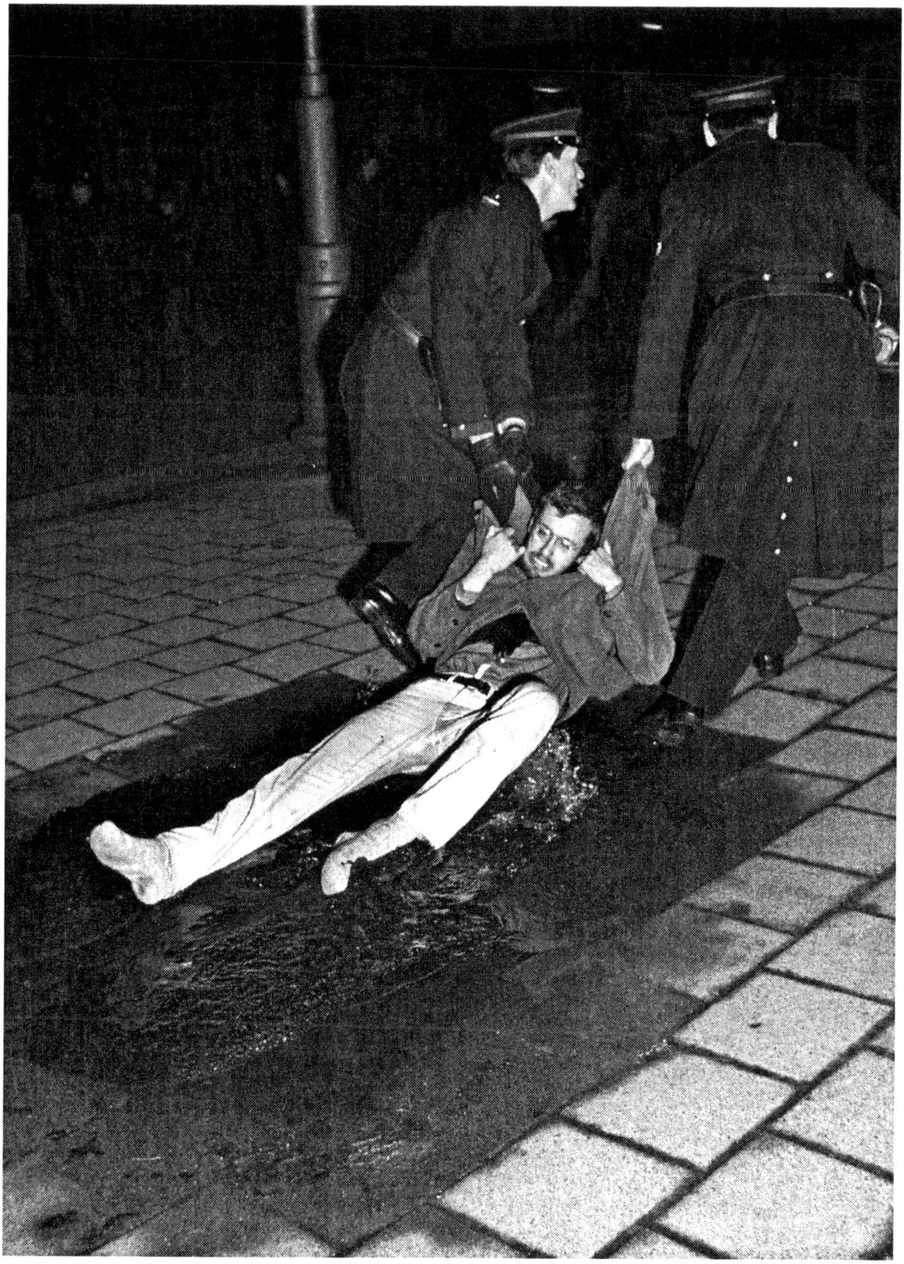

Provo Hans Metz being dragged through a puddle of water by the Amsterdam Police at an anti-Vietnam War demonstration in front of the American Consulate.

on other Provos continued. On April 16th, Peter Bronkhorst was arrested "on suspicion of giving a speech." He drew a fine of 75 guilders. Two Provos were arrested for setting a fire between the legs of the Lieverdje statue, but were freed the next day. In reaction to the situation, a meeting of some forty Provos decided to participate in the June 1st municipal elections. An older generation of pre-Provo anarchists opposed the decision, as did Harry Mulisch, for they saw in it the end of Provo as the original and creative street-based anarchist movement it had been. But those who had attended the meeting stood by their decision.

There are 45 seats on the Amsterdam Dutch *Gemeenteraad* (City Council) — the size of the council for each city or town depends on the size of the population. During community elections each party draws up a list of candidates in their order of preference. Voters vote for specific candidates, and individual candidates on the party list are elected in proportion to the percentage of the vote that the party receives at-large. For instance, a party receiving 15% of the vote would get seven seats on the council (15% of 45). The candidates have a lot to do with what makes the party attractive to the voters, but the seats belong to the party. Should anyone elected to a seat give up that seat, it is filled by the next person on the list of the party.

The Provos chose thirteen candidates for their list. The first name was student journalist, Bernhard De Vries, from *Propria Cures*, who had joined Provo shortly before the events of March 10th. He was handsome and showed promise as a political leader. Irene Donner-Van der Wetering, an active feminist and one of the originators of Provo's White Wives Plan, was second on the list. At the time of the election meeting, she had been a Provo for only a week. These two were believed to be the most attractive to voters should Provo have any success at the polls. But also on the list was Jef Last, a 68 year-old Dutch writer and hagiographer of Andre Gide; Constant Nieuwenhuys, the COBRA artist who developed the New Babylon plan (*see* Appendix 1); and Roel Van Duyn. Van Duyn had strongly supported having the Provos participate in the election, saying that by running candidates they would be able to get the judiciary and the police off their backs. He claims that he was not placed high on the list (only #5) so as to avoid the label of "leader." But other commentators have averred that he was removed from the top of the original list against his will.

Although Mulisch did not approve of Provo participation in the elections, he did vote for them. Having gone this far, he felt that they now needed to win or the police and the judiciary would react harshly. According to Mulisch, they worked hard in their print shop, day and night. Their posters were up all over Amsterdam, on every corner and on bridges that crossed the canals. Guards were mounted to watch the posters because right-wingers and admiring collectors kept tearing them down.

An idea of the Provo campaign platform can be gained from the brochure, *Wat de Provos willen (What The Provos Want)*, which Duco Van Weerlee had written a month earlier. Although the main Provo slogan was "VOTE PROVO FOR BETTER WEATHER," a fabulous idea for rain-soaked Holland, there was much serious intent in their campaign, including the following White Plans:

> The White Bicycle Plan: In an effort to address traffic congestion in the center of the city, white bicycles would become the common property of all the people of Amsterdam. Automobiles would be excluded from the center of the city.
>
> The White Chimney Plan: A mandate that chimneys have special built-in incinerators to combat air pollution; with fines for infractions.
>
> The White Chicken Plan: Amsterdam's police force should be recast as unarmed friendly social workers with candy and band-aids in their pockets.
>
> The White Dwelling Plan: In an effort to ease the city's housing shortage the city government would publish a weekly list of empty buildings so people without homes could squat them.
>
> The White Wives Plan: Developed by Irene Donner-Van der Wetering, this plan called for sex education for young people. Among other things it mandated information on contraception, medical clinics for young girls, and teaching family planning.
>
> The White Schools Plan: Students would have a say in expanding opportunities for democratically organized study and discussion.
>
> The White City Plan: Amsterdam would become the first urban area committed to implementing Constant Nieuwenhuis' New Babylon. (See Appendix 1)

In addition to the White Plans, Provo had other suggestions. The Royal Palace, which was built on the site of a city hall that had burned down in the 17th century, would once again become the City Hall. It would be returned to the people. The Van Heutsz statue, a monument to colonial militarism, would be demolished. Every effort should be made to prevent depopulation of the center city. Citizens must have the right to freely hold Happenings, and the streets should become a play area. Mayor Van Hall should go on permanent leave.

The Provo program was technocratic in nature, tied to the idea of Amsterdam as a cultural playground for a society where the bulk of labor would be performed by computers. Although parts of it might seem unfeasible or perhaps reformist in character, the program as a whole presented a clear vision of how to reorder civic life.

On April 23rd Koosje Koster, a female student who was number six on the Provo electoral list, was arrested at the Lieverdje for passing out raisins to passersby. At the police station she refused to

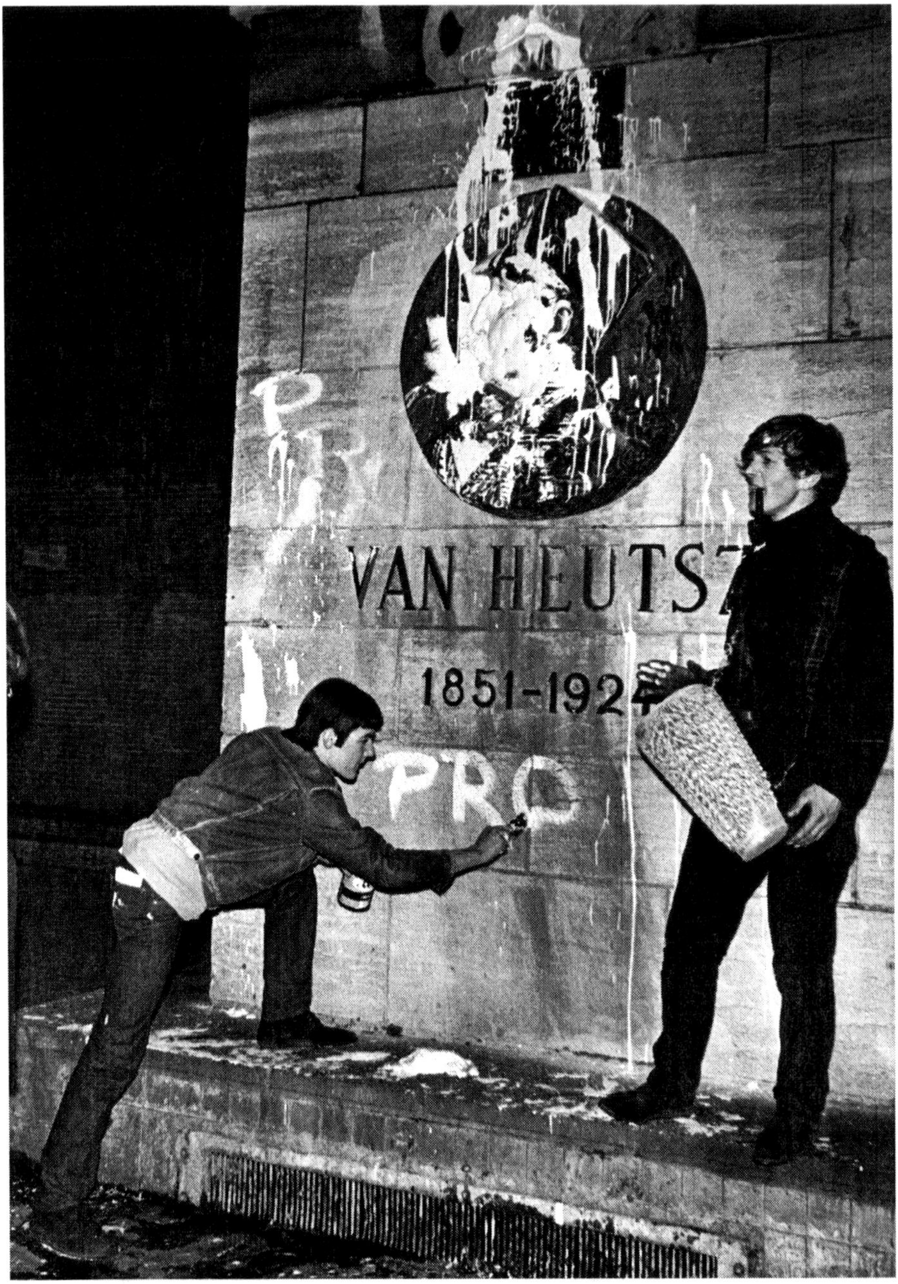

Auke Boersma (on left), painting the Van Heutsz Monument white. Van Heutsz was the Dutch general who subdued the native forces in colonizing the Dutch East Indies (present-day Indonesia). The monument was a favorite Provo target because of its political implications. White is, of course, the color that represents Provo.

allow a policewoman to undress her. This was a normal procedure, which the police justified as a means of preventing suicide. However, they did not explain that to her at the time. When she continued to resist, three male officers assisted in disrobing her, allowing her to keep only her underwear. She was wrapped in a blanket during the lengthy police hearing afterward. Koster was released the day after her arrest on probation, and her account of the incident varied considerably from that of the police. On April 27th Van Hall told the city council that it was unfeasible even to try to prevent a repetition of such acts, that the rule requiring prisoners to undress was absolutely necessary as a deterrent to suicide. Nevertheless, the Koster incident became a prominent symbol of police insensitivity during the growing political crisis.

The Saturday night following Koster's release, there was more rioting on the Spui. At 11:45 P.M., about 400 people gathered at the Lieverdje. A car seat soaked in gasoline was set on fire at the base of the statue and people danced in a circle around it. Then plainclothes police moved in and made arrests. Uniformed officers tried to disperse the crowd, arresting those who refused to comply. Fights broke out between the police and the crowd. When the police finally left, the remaining people tried to organize another Happening. This prolonged tension for several more hours into the night.

Cor Jaring, a freelance photographer who had won Grootveld's confidence in 1965, had become the unofficial "court photographer" of the Happening scene. He documented this Happening, as well as a more general history of everything that was occurring in Amsterdam before the June 1966 elections. Earlier in the day he had helped two English television journalists who were making a film about the Provos. He led them to the Provo boat and the Provo press, which was set up in the basement of the home of the avant-garde Dutch composer, Peter Schat. But when they tried to video the activity at the Leidseplein the police chased them away. To escape, Jaring, the two Englishmen, a Dutch photographer, and a Dutch cameraman jogged down the Leidsestraat, away from the Leidseplein in the direction of both the Lieverdje and the Dam. When they reached the Koningsplein, near the Lieverdje, the *Rijkspolitie* (national police) had closed the street and waved them back toward the local police.

The five journalists found themselves closed off on two sides by more than 200 policemen, but were ordered to keep moving. Though there wasn't a Provo in sight, the police began hitting both Jaring and cameraman, Piet Van Strien. Dutch photographer Wim Van Rossum was beaten badly by two policemen. Jaring was wearing a polyester shield on his back, under his clothing. As the police beat him they heard hollow sounds that they were unable to understand. Keeping to the sides of the buildings so that he would only be hit from one side, Jaring was able to break through the wall of policemen by shoving one of them aside and making a run for the Singel canal.

At this point the Rijkspolitie was diverted by a group of Provos coming over the bridge from the direction of the Lieverdje. Jaring and his colleagues were able to escape with the Provos, but Van Rossum could barely move. When one of the fleeing Provos fell, about twenty of them tumbled over one another. Jaring rolled under a car and the other four members of his party kept running. From his hiding place, he witnessed two dozen policemen beating the twenty fallen Provos. The beating lasted five minutes, and when the victims finally managed to stumble away, three of them remained unconscious on the street; Jaring later visited them in the hospital. Many Amsterdammers were beginning to resent the constant police abuse, and related to the Provos' position. Although Mayor Van Hall said that it was the teenagers who were responsible for the rioting, Jaring notes that only a small minority of them deliberately provoked riots. But they were determined and, given the police attitude, he predicted, Amsterdam was due for a major riot.

April 30th was Queen Juliana's birthday, a national holiday in the Netherlands. The Orange-Committee, Pearl of the Jordaan, decided to host a provotarian celebration that would include a White Bicycle marathon on the Dam, where the bicycles would circle the Royal Palace. Then there would be a beauty contest for "Miss Provo-Chick, 1966." (Princess Beatrix and her sisters were invited to compete for the title.) And following the beauty contest would come a "Butter, cheese, and egg throwing tournament" between the police and the Provos. There would also be an auction of the rare 1st and 7th issues of *Provo* — rare because most of the print run had been seized by the police — and the festivities would finish with a smoke-bomb-throwing competition.

The day's events began at the Lieverdje, where a recorder ensemble called the Provonadu Orchestra performed. After that the crowd moved to the Leidseplein to dump lemonade powder into the fountain on the square. Members of a fascist group called *Jong Europa* (Young Europe), who tried leafleting the crowd, soon joined the lemonade powder in the Leidseplein fountain. The celebrants then moved on to the Huis van Bewaring where Hans Tuynman was incarcerated to hold a sit-in demonstration. During the official program on the Dam, a two-year-old girl was chosen to be Miss Provo-Chick, 1966. Only when Auka Boersma presented the White Housing Plan at the vacant Royal Palace, advocating for squatters' rights, did the police began making arrests. The arrests continued far into the night.

IN HOLLAND STAAT UN HUIS

EN IN DAT HUIS
WOONT NIEMAND
HET STAAT OP DE DAM
IN HET HART VAN AMSTERDAM
HET PALEIS OP DE DAM IS
HET IMAGE VAN DE WONINGNOOD
IN AMSTERDAM STAAN DUIZENDEN HUIZEN LEEG LANGS
DE GRACHTENGORDEL EN IN DE JORDAAN, HET
AMSTERDAMSE BOLWERK VAN DE VRYHEID Q

UW HUIS IS UW GNOT-
TEMPEL. U HEEFT
RECHT OP UN EIGEN
HUIS EN UN RECHT-
VAARDIGE VERDELING
VAN HET KOLLEKTIEF
WONINGBEZIT. GEEN
HUIS IN HET MAGIES
CENTRUM MAG WOR-
DEN AFGEBROKEN
ZOLANG ER NOG
MENSEN IN WONEN
NEW AMSTERDAM

PROVO'S WERKGROEP
WITTE HUIZENPLAN LAN
SEERT UN LIEVEREVO-
LUSIONAIRE OPLOS
SING VAN HET WO-
NINGPROBLEEM .HET
WITTE HUIS IN HET
WITTE HUIS KAN IE-
DEREEN BINNEN-
GAAN EN ZYN WOON
RUIMTE UITZOEKEN
NEW BABYLON

HET WITTE HUIZEN PLAN

DE WERKGROEP WITTE HUIZENPLAN NAM DE VOLGENDE INITIATIEVEN:
① Het UITROEPEN VAN HET PALEIS OP DE DAM TOT STADHUIS VAN
AMSTERDAM de KOLLEKTIEVE KLAOSTEMPEL VAN HET MAGIES CENTRUM
②De WEKELYKSE UITGAVE VAN UN LYST MET ADRESSEN VAN LEEG—
STAANDE HUIZEN DIE'SZATERDAGS OM 10 UUR OP DE DAM VERSPREID WORDT
③HET WITSCHILDEREN VAN DE DEUR EN DEURPOST VAN LEEGSTAANDE
WONINGEN TEN TEKEN DAT IEDEREEN ERIN WONEN KAN
④DE OPRICHTING VAN UN ARBEIDSBUREAU OM DE JONGEREN IN DE
ZOMERMAANDEN TE MOBILISEREN TEGEN DE WONINGNOOD
⑤HET WITTE HUIZENPLAN ZAL DEEL UITMAKEN VAN HET PLAN NEW AMSTERDAM

REDTUN PANDJE BEZE TUN PAN DJE - GNOTWILHET

Flyer explaining the White House Plan. Translation: THERE IS A HOUSE IN HOLLAND And nobody lives there. It stands in the Dam square in the heart of Amsterdam. The Palace on the Dam is a symbol of the housing shortage. In Amsterdam there are thousands of empty houses around the canals and in the Jordaan, the city's bastion of freedom. Your house is your pleasure temple. You have a right to your own house, a fair share of the community's housing. No house in the Magic Centre can be allowed to be demolished if it is still being occupied. New Amsterdam!

The Provo 'White House Plan' workshop puts forward a grand revolutionary solution to the housing problem—'The White House'. Anyone can enter the White House and choose his own apartment. New Babylon!

THE WHITE HOUSE PlAN The White House Plan workshop has taken the following steps: 1. declaring the Palace on the Dam the Town Hall, the collective Klaas temple of the Magic Centre;

2. publishing every week a list of addresses of empty houses for distribution on saturday mornings at 10 in the Dam square;

3. painting the doors and doorposts of empty houses white to indicate that anyone can use them;

4. founding an employment agency to mobilize young people in the summer months to combat the housing shortage;

5. The White House Plan will form part of the New Amsterdam Plan.

SAVE A BUILDING OCCUPY A BUILDING JUST FOR FUN

May 5th is the anniversary of the Netherlands' liberation from the Nazi occupation in World War II. By then, demonstrations had become a daily occurrence. A Vietnam Action Group had been formed to stage anti-Vietnam War demonstrations on the third Sunday of every month. (At the first demonstration there were hundreds of arrests.) Likewise, every Saturday night demonstrators protested the imprisonment of Hans Tuynman. The earliest of these demonstrations in support of Tuynman marched from the Lieverdje to the prison on the Amstelveenseweg, but later ones set off from the Leidseplein. Harry Mulisch describes them as "mass guerilla theater." The crowds dispersed under police pressure, then regrouped elsewhere. Marchers played wooden flutes and clapped their hands to the chant of "Tuyn-Man-Free! Tuyn-Man-Free!" The sidewalks of the demonstration routes were crowded with spectators and the busy Amstelveenseweg, in front of the prison, was jammed with blocked automobiles.

Throughout the month of May, the Provo phenomenon spread to other Dutch cities. There were arrests at the Geis statue in Maastricht, capital of the province of Limburg. Auke Boersma was jailed for five days for violating his probation when he climbed a statue in Dordrecht, a city in the province of South Holland. On May 14th, in Rotterdam, sixteen people were arrested at the Fikkie statue, and on May 21st, twenty-two more were arrested in Rotterdam during a demonstration.

But it was Amsterdam, of course, that remained the focus of Provo activity. On May 7th, eleven people were arrested on the Spui. On May 16th, nine demonstrators were arrested during a sit-in at the home of the American Consul-General in Amsterdam. On May 21st, ten people were arrested at an Amsterdam Happening. On May 26th, as a result of police misconduct during a protest demonstration against the colonial war in Angola at the Portuguese legation in Amsterdam, three complaints were filed against the police. On May 29th, Ite Hamming and another Provo were arrested and held for five days for driving a truck plastered with political slogans around the Leidseplein. On May 30th nine Provos, including Koosje Koster, now an official Provo candidate for City Council, were arrested for carrying a White Whale made of air mattresses and sheets into the center of Amsterdam. Then, on May 31st, Koster was arrested again for posting Provo campaign literature, for which she was sentenced to five days for violating her April 24th probation (when she was forcibly undressed). Irene Donner-Van der Wetering, the number two candidate on the Provo list, was arrested on June 1st, the night of the municipal elections, along with NTS (Netherlands Television) editor Van der Linde. Both were held overnight. The executive committee of the Amsterdam Press Club

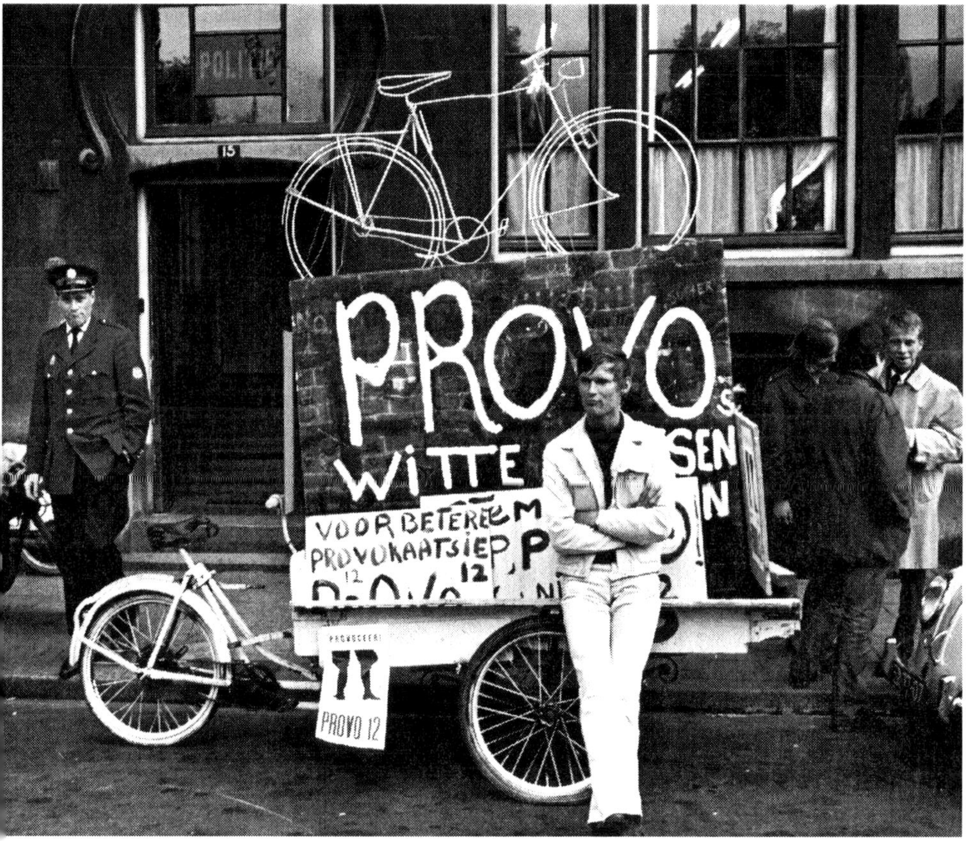

Bernhard de Vries campaigning for the Provo party for the June 1966 Amsterdam municipal elections. Partially visible is a sign, mounted on the *bakfiets,* that translates "Vote Provo for Better Weather," a winning slogan in the rain-soaked Netherlands. De Vries headed the Provo list and won their only seat on the Amsterdam City Council.

filed a protest with the ministries of Justice and Interior on behalf of Van der Linde, and he was officially told to keep his distance from any place in Amsterdam where disturbances might take place. The press protested that this prohibition would hinder the professional operation of journalists.

Harry Mulisch's sharp reaction to the tide of events in Amsterdam was typical of a fairly large segment of the population. Until now, he said, judges had been believed to be unprejudiced interpreters of the law whose interest in seeing that justice was served was above any expression of personal bias. Now people were debating which of the various judges were worse than the others, and who was worst of all. They were all imposing a system of caste justice, with different standards for the Provos and their sympathizers than for other citizens who passed through the courts.

Mulisch's insight was especially well illustrated by the TRES case. TRES was an exclusive fraternity at the University of Utrecht whose membership came from the nobility. In May of 1966, a young man died as a result of his fraternity initiation. The two young noblemen held responsible for his death were merely given small fines, which contrasted sharply with the treatment reserved by the court for the Provos. The unusually mild sentences prompted protests throughout the country, and eventually the guilty aristocrats were re-sentenced to prison terms.

Yet another section of the Amsterdam bureaucracy sought to profit from the international interest in the Provos. The VVV, the Dutch national tourist office, published a brochure entitled *See the Provos*, which was distributed in local hotels. Interested tourists were driven to Enkhuizen, a picturesque 17th-century port an hour north of Amsterdam, where for a fee they were provoked by government-sanctioned "Provos."

Nevertheless, neither the reversal of the TRES decision nor the official attempts to market the Provos to outsiders altered the violent tactics that the police continued employing on the streets of Amsterdam. In May, Mulisch and Ed Hoornik, another Dutch writer, were attacked by police during a protest near the Spui. Elsewhere, police were beating up teenagers and dragging them into the police stations. At a time when one could go to prison for passing out leaflets, no one was safe from imprisonment. One demonstration against the Vietnam War almost came off peacefully. One common charge for arrest was "insulting a friendly chief-of-state," which was brought whenever someone shouted "Johnson *Mordenaar*!" (Johnson Murderer), referring to Lyndon Johnson. But at this demonstration, no one shouted. Nor did the demonstrators carry any banners with slogans that Van Hall could object to. As a police report, dated May 15th, 1966 described it, 500 people marched silently through the center of the city, carrying flowers, obeying traffic regulations, and keeping to the sidewalks. At the Dam, they placed their flowers on the National Monument. But then a group of noisy, yelling Provos moved into the Kalverstraat heading for the Museumplein behind the Rijksmuseum to stage a sit-in at the American consulate. Nine of them were arrested, so the remaining demonstrators headed for the Hilton Hotel where they pulled a flag to half-mast and the crowd was dispersed by the police.

It should be stressed that many of the Provo-sanctioned demonstrations were part of their election strategy. They were clever political theater designed to garner publicity and public sympathy. A fine example of this was when Bernhard De Vries, the #1 Provo candidate for the City Council, was arrested on May 24th during a carefully staged (and deliberately unsuccessful) attempt to free Hans Tuynman from prison. De Vries was charged with trespassing. In his possession were a firecracker, a broken radio, a map of Spain, a floor plan of the prison, and a long length of rope.

When Amsterdam's municipal elections were finally held on June 1st, there were rock bands playing at a tent set up for dancing on the Amstelveld. Expectations were high, but the final results had Provo winning only one seat on the City Council, that of Bernhard De Vries. The news was ruefully accepted by the provotariat, which had been seriously hoping for three or four seats. However, given that the voting age in the Netherlands at the time was 23, Provo popularity was not easily translated into electoral victory.

The Provos displayed their continuing strength immediately after the election with another demonstration on behalf of Hans Tuynman at the House of Detention. This time, Professor Van den Berg, Professor of Roman Law at the University of Nijmegen, contributed by protesting the practice of suspending due process of law for anyone on probation. Support for Tuynman also came from a young member of the central committee of the large Dutch Socialist Party, Jan Nagel. Nagel was representative of the new development in the *Partij van de Arbeid* (Socialist Party), the *Nieuwe Links* (New Left) which eventually took it in a more truly Socialist direction. Though 850 intellectuals signed a petition against the behavior of the police and the judiciary, only the two Socialist dailies, *Het Vrije Volk* and *Het Parool* (after considerable hedging) would publish it. The other newspapers refused. Fifty of the signers paid 500 guilders and names continued to come in. Harry Mulisch was active in organizing the petition, but its importance was quickly diminished by other events.

Ominously, during the night of June 13th, the word MOORD (Murder) appeared in blue letters six feet high on the National Monument on the Dam. It was as if a veil had suddenly been lifted from the façade of respectability serving to cloak the injustices upon which society is built, shattered by a word. The people of Amsterdam, walking the streets of their city, were about to transform into combatants and the streets into battlefields.

works referenced

Commissee voor Onzerzoek Amsterdam (1967), pp. 2–3; Duyn (1967); Hall (1976); Jaring (1968); Mulisch (1967); Scheepmaker (1967), pp. 15-16; Singer (1970); Sinner (1966); Tuynman (1968); Weerlee (1966).

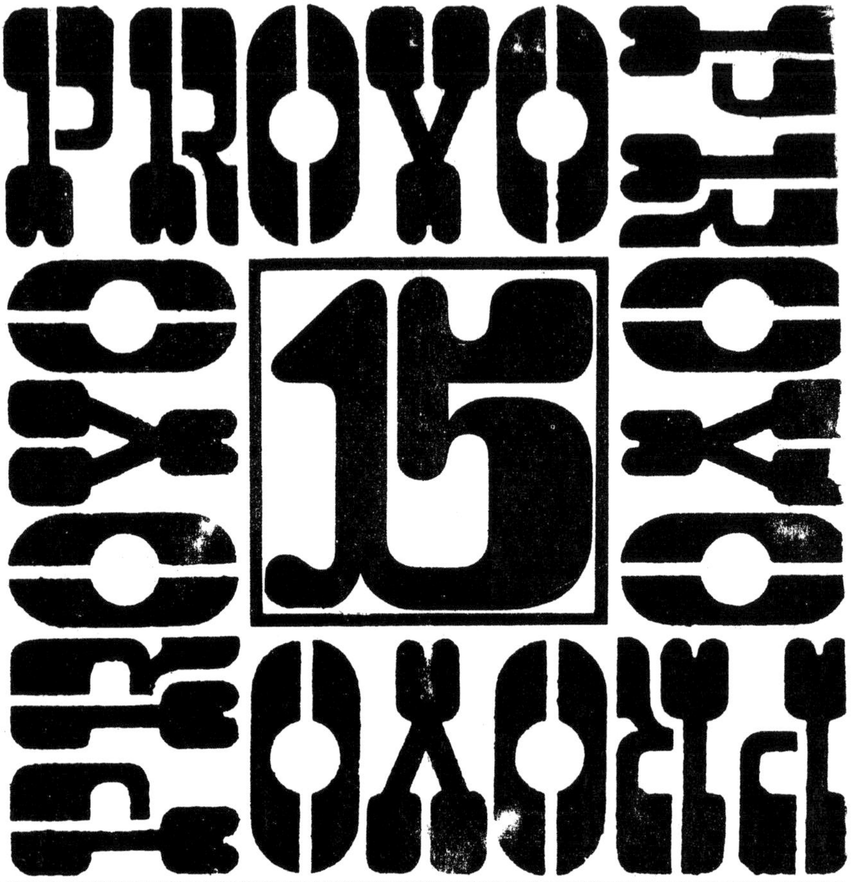

DIT IS PROVO 15 - Provo kost los *f* 1,-- Abonnement *f* 10 of *f* 12 of nog meer
MAART - Provo verschijnt maandelijks - Provopost naar Postbus 1602 (zegel ins
Poen naar EN LET NU OP GVD: postgiro 750734 tnv J.J. Ham, gem. giro P 9200
Telefoon 236453 & 231654

Provo is een blad voor dubbelspionnen, persvogels, kommissarissen, aandeelhouders, direkteuren, uitvinders, straatvegers, dakdekkers, fotografen, lassers, aristokraten,brandkastenkrakers,telefielen, homofielen, heterofielen, cinefiele autofielen,voetbalfielen,profielen, open-deuren-intrappers,progressieve dominee soosjologen, psiegologen, frietverkopers, residifisten, trotskisten, oubollige oude heertjes, schoenpoetsers, politieke delinkwenten, burokraten, N.V.S.H.ers, K N.A.C.ers, A.N.W.Bers, PeevdAers, P.S.J.Wers, S.J.ers, C.B.H.ers, K.N.Z.H.V.M K.N.L.T.B.ers Pleebeejers, anglofoben, kleptomanen, psiegopaten en ander gespl persoonlijkheden.

The cover of *Provo #15*. Translation: *Provo* is a paper for counterintelligence agents, paparazzi, commissars, shareholders, CEOs, inventors, street sweepers, roofers, photographers, welders, aristocrats, safecrackers, telephiles, homophiles, heterophiles, cinephiles, autophiles, soccer fans, profile lovers [*profilen*, a pun], open-door intruders, progressive clergy, sociologists, psychologists, french fry vendors, recidivists, Trotskyites, droll old fellows, shoeshine boys, political delinquents, bureaucrats, [this is followed by a number of organizational acronyms, such as] the Netherlands Society for Sexual Reform, the Royal Netherlands Autonomobile Club, the Socialist Party, Socialist Youth members, plebeians, Anglophobes, kleptomaniacs, psychopaths and other split personalities.

7. the monster of amsterdam (june 14, 1966)

The Provos were not the only people in Amsterdam with grievances against authority. Though they and their Dada-style political theatrics had so far made the most impact on the structures of power, it was a jest of cosmic irony that the capital of the Netherlands was eventually brought to the brink of civil war over a minor labor dispute. A 2% cut in the vacation allowance of unorganized construction workers in Amsterdam had been mandated to pay the administrative costs of handling their vacations. The issue underlying the workers' response to the cut was the same one the Provos faced: authoritarianism. The decision had been made at the national level of the trade union movement without any discussion of the issue with the workers themselves, and without putting it to a vote. As a result, all of Amsterdam's construction workers simply said "No!"

So by early June of 1966 the structure of authority in the Netherlands was set to be challenged by the same explosive combination of workers and youth that would rock France during the dynamic revolution of May 1968. Roel Van Duyn was stating the obvious when he wrote that the generalized tension resulting from the government's overreaction to Provo activity needed little fuel in order to take fire.

The most accessible source on the Battle of Amsterdam, as the riots generated by the labor dispute quickly became known, is a 90-page booklet entitled *Oproer in Amsterdam (Revolt in Amsterdam). Oproer* was written by reporters from De Telegraaf and slants editorially in favor of the police. From time to time it takes snide digs at both the workers and at various government officials, most of whom were members of the Dutch Socialist Party. Nonetheless, it does capture the essence and chaos of the June 14th riots, being in part a summary of a long official document, the *Interim Report of the Commission for Research on the Amsterdam Incidents*, created by the Dutch parliament during its investigation of the riots and the circumstances that led to them. The three-volume published report is verbose in official language but richly documents its case with depositions from dozens of witnesses.

Monday the 13th of June had started as a warm workday morning. But beneath the serene countenance of the weather the turbulent events of the past few months were gathering for a full-fledged storm. At 1:00 P.M. on Saturday, the Leidseplein had been in a state of siege. For the first time assembly had been forbidden at the popular square. The police had been criticized from both sides for their changing tactics in dealing with Provo disturbances, which had vacillated between an approach that was far too harsh and another that was lenient. *Oproer in Amsterdam* concludes that the ongoing criticism ultimately short-circuited both Mayor Van Hall and Police Chief Van der Molen, the two officials responsible for directing Amsterdam's police force. In July 1965, on the occasion of their first official visit, Van Hall had told Princess Beatrix and Claus von Amsberg that "Amsterdam is a recalcitrant city and Amsterdammers are a recalcitrant people, but that is perhaps because the heart of the Netherlands beats most strongly there." *Oproer in Amsterdam* and contemporary reports in *De Telegraaf* all stress that the mayor never seemed secure as the principle authority in the city and that his policy was to avoid pitched battle at any cost.

The organized construction workers were to be reimbursed for the 2% cut in their vacation pay by their trade unions, but 70% of Amsterdam's construction trade was unorganized and a majority of the workers was Communist. Those workers would have to pay the new administrative costs out of pocket. A month earlier the C.P.N. (Dutch Communist Party) had launched a major campaign against the unfair ruling. The party newspaper, *De Waarheid (The Truth)*, termed it "wage theft." On that warm Monday morning of June 13th, the Communists distributed pamphlets calling for a demonstration that evening at the St. Elizabeth Patronaat on the Marnixstraat at the far edge of the Jordaan district. There the unions intended to make their first reimbursement payments to organized members whose last names began with "A" or "B."

Jan Weggelaar, a 51-year-old construction worker, wore slippers to the demonstration because he lived nearby. This casual act, so typical of the way Amsterdammers lived at that time, was lost in the impact of his death less than an hour later; a death that plunged the city into a state of civil war. At noon Chief Inspector Brouwer of the Amsterdam Police spoke with leaders of the three construction unions. He had anticipated trouble from the unorganized workers after seeing the Communist pamphlets, but he acceded to a request from the union leaders to send only plainclothes police to observe the payments that evening.

Brouwer arrived at the Marnixstraat site at 7:10 P.M. — payments were to begin at 8:00. Small knots of men waited for the St. Elizabeth hall to open. Because of the prevailing calm, Brouwer told his men that he felt they had been called out for nothing. By 7:20 the crowd was growing. There was still no sign of trouble, but the Mobile Unit, the riot police, was on hand at police headquarters, and a Volkswagen van of four men was on reserve at a nearby station. By 7:25 the crowd was blocking traffic on the busy Marnixstraat. The four officers in the van were called in at 7:30 to direct traffic, and arrived at 7:45. By then the crowd numbered between 600 and 700 men. The demonstrators immediately surrounded the police van and tension began to mount. Brouwer pulled his men back from the crowd, deciding to have them direct traffic from a short distance away, but the traffic was too heavy for four men to handle. The Mobile Unit, which consisted of 30 officers led by Chief Inspector Wit, was called in. By the time the Mobile Unit arrived, the crowd numbered over a thousand men. *Oproer in Amsterdam* called it a crowd ripe for a riot.

Speaking through a Mobile Unit megaphone, Wit ordered the crowd to disperse. When his words were lost in the pandemonium, *Oproer in Amsterdam* reports that he tried speaking personally to some of the demonstrators. It isn't clear what he said, but suddenly there was an impromptu sit-down on the Marnixstraat and three men began hitting him. They took his hat. Wit drew his club and ordered his men to do likewise. The fight lasted only five minutes. It was over before 8:00, ending as quickly as it began. The result: a draw.

As the police regrouped they heard shouts: "Someone is dead!" *Oproer* claims that Jan Weggelaar suffered a heart attack and was lying in the street before the fighting began. (Someone had mumbled something to that effect within Inspector Wit's range of hearing.) The question of his heart attack soon became moot as an excuse justifying either side's actions during the next 24 hours. In a broader perspective, as Harry Mulisch observes, it was beside the point to establish exactly what happened. For all practical purposes (and effects) the police appeared to have murdered a man. Amsterdam had been on the brink of a riot for months and Jan Weggelaar's death tipped the balance toward a major battle.

An ambulance arrived to pick up the body. Wit and Brouwer retreated, the police beating their way through the crowd. They took a wounded demonstrator with them, a man injured by a cobblestone. The demonstration moved from the Marnixstraat via the Rozengracht towards the Stadhuis (City Hall). Wit contacted Police Commissioner Molenkamp, who tried without success to telephone Mayor Van Hall, who was visiting friends that evening. When Molenkamp couldn't reach Van Hall, he called Deputy-Mayor Van Wijck, who refused to take responsibility for command of the police in the Mayor's absence.

Dr. A. P. Van der Weij, a physician who lived across the street from the Wilhemina Gasthuis, a large Amsterdam hospital, was asked to help treat the wounded construction workers. Van der Weij was the first doctor to see Jan Weggelaar's body. He had heard from other construction workers that Weggelaar had been beaten, so he was surprised to find no signs of violence. In speaking to Weggelaar's father, the doctor guessed that Weggelaar might have died of a broken neck. However, an autopsy conducted by a Dr. Wagenvoort at the request of the Judicial Commissioner showed no evidence of either violence or a broken neck. Dr. Zeldenrust, the judicial physician, conveniently concurred with Wagenvoort's report.

At 8:30 P.M. Molenkamp reached Police Chief Van der Molen at home and informed him of the situation. When he arrived at police headquarters Van der Molen was astonished to find Inspector Wit arming his Mobile Unit with carbines, helmets, and tear gas grenades in order to head off the demonstrators. Van der Molen put a stop to those preparations in hopes of forestalling more deaths. More high-ranking police officials arrived, but no one was able to contact Van Hall. At this point it still seemed possible that the situation might be resolved by a meeting between the Mayor and the leadership of the unorganized construction workers. With an escort of just 10 policemen Van der Molen drove to the Stadhuis in uniform and tried to reason with the leaders. A go-between set up a meeting, but only after Van der Molen agreed to dismiss two police vehicles in the area. During the course of the meeting the heated emotions of the day seemed to cool and the demonstrators asked to meet someone from the City Council. Several City Councilors met with the strike leaders, and one of them informed the police chief that the construction workers would be meeting at the Dokwerker Monument the next day at 10:00 A.M. to decide whether or not to walk off the job. Only at 11:30 P.M., when he returned home, was Mayor Van Hall finally apprised of the evening's events. By midnight, all was quiet at the Stadhuis, and he considered the incident closed. No one expected any violence the following day.

The press conference on Jan Weggelaar's death took place at 1:30 A.M. *Oproer in Amsterdam* notes that the lateness of the hour resulted in the city edition of *De Telegraaf*, which appeared at midnight, carrying the inaccurate report that Weggelaar's death had been caused by other demonstrators. The paper paid dearly for that story. Later that night Amsterdam was quiet, save for a few Provos who shouted "Murderers!" at police headquarters but retreated to the Leidseplein when chased away. By 4:30 A.M., all policemen not usually on duty had been sent home.

crisis at *de telegraaf*

At 9:00 A.M. on June 14th a crowd began gathering at the Dokwerker Monument. By 9:45 it was estimated to number 5,000. Police Chief Van der Molen hadn't arrived at police headquarters until 8:45. (In a later statement he explained that he thought all the problems had been resolved the night before.) When the City Council met to discuss the situation, Van der Molen expected general acceptance of the fact that Jan Weggelaar died of a heart attack rather than as a result of police brutality. He told the Council that it was pointless to ask for reinforcements from the national government in The Hague. Firstly, more uniformed men might incite a worse riot; and secondly, the Minister of Interior was not supportive of the situation in Amsterdam and had turned down previous requests for reinforcements.

When he got to the Central Police Station Van der Molen phoned Mayor Van Hall and asked to meet with him at his office to discuss the previous evening's riot. At 9:30 A.M. he walked from the station to the Stadhuis. Before he left he told Chief Commissioner Hammega, the ranking officer on duty, that he could be reached at the Mayor's Office, and explicitly said that the Mobile Unit was not to be deployed save on his personal order. Hammega assumed that Van der Molen had discussed the matter with Van Hall and that the order originated from the Mayor. The direct order blocked the Amsterdam police from taking initiative, should a disturbance occur. Van der Molen didn't foresee any problems arising because of his absence: he could easily be reached by phone.

After their meeting, Van Hall asked Van der Molen to remain in order to discuss police reinforcements with the Procurer-General (the Attorney General) for the province of North Holland. Among those present was P. J. P. Hoogenboom, the Mayor's advisor on political affairs. News of the demonstration at the Dokwerker and the subsequent movement of the construction workers in the direction of *De Telegraaf* office reached the Mayor's Office just before the meeting began at 10:00 A.M.

In analyzing this moment in the gestation of the conflict it is tempting to see Robert Jasper Grootveld's famous "Klaas" effect manifesting once again, this time in the unwitting person of Klaas Staphorst, the Communist trade union leader. *Oproer* gives a vivid, perhaps overly dramatic, description of the workers' rally at the Dokwerker Monument, claiming that tempers were fanned by Staphorst's inflammatory oratory. Many workers had armed themselves with tools and barrel staves, and Staphorst reportedly said of *De Telegraaf*: "I could do without that paper for a while." The crowd set fire to copies of the paper, which by now was reporting the "correct information" about Weggelaar dying a natural death.

Chief Inspector A. M. Koppejan of the police station at the nearby Meijerplein had given permission for the Dokwerker demonstration to two members of the Construction Workers Action Committee. He had further agreed to limit the use of policemen to directing traffic away from the Meijerplein square: union representatives said that they could manage the crowd and that more policemen would only incite the workers and inflame the situation. When the crowd began getting unruly, Koppejan had only a few men on duty and almost no reserves.

The riot ignited spontaneously. One group of workers attacked the nearby offices of the *Sociaal Fonds van de Bouwnijverheid* (Social Pension Funds of the Construction Industry), the organization that had mandated the 2% cut in vacation pay. Amidst a shower of splintering glass, the organization director, J. M. de Roy van Zuydewijn, phoned the police station at the Meijerplein and was told that the police couldn't spare any extra men. Two policemen had already been roughed up by the crowd. Twelve windows were broken before the crowd dispersed without attempting to force entry into the building. The rioters had another target in mind.

As the mob poured out of the Meijerplein they yelled, "On to *De Telegraaf*!" Two reporters covering the demonstration for the paper called the news chief, Otto Kuijk, to warn of the onslaught. Kuijk called his security chief and told him to take precautions against a possible attack. At 10:00 A.M., the security chief phoned the police but could get no promise of immediate assistance. Kuijk informed *De Telegraaf*'s managing editor, C. J. Brandt, of the situation. While in Brandt's office he received a phone call from Police Inspector Romeijn, who promised to keep the *Telegraaf* building under surveillance and requested to be kept informed of any further news.

A crowd of 120 mostly non-union construction workers reached the offices of *De Telegraaf* at 10:40 A.M. The security chief sounded the emergency siren and iron gates closed off the main entrance — the side doors and larger windows were protected by metal shutters. There wasn't a single policeman in sight. The rioters shattered the windows on the lower floors with bricks from a nearby building site — a *Telegraaf* reporter was hit by a brick and taken to hospital. Then a passing streetcar was stopped in its tracks, its front windows were broken and its driver was shoved from the vehicle. The driver managed to evade capture and moments later made a getaway in the streetcar.

Debris of the *Telegraaf* trucks.

Several demonstrators climbed onto the shipping dock and did what damage they could. Another group knocked over one of the paper's large delivery trucks, which fell on top of a parked car. A bonfire of copies of the paper was soon blazing in the middle of the street, the Nieuwe Zijds Voorburgwal. One demonstrator parked a second *Telegraaf* vehicle on the streetcar tracks. The newspapers inside were unloaded and set on fire, and the vehicle was repositioned over the flames. It exploded. When two fire engines arrived they were blocked by the crowd. More automobiles were damaged. Under cover of a shower of bricks demonstrators tried to force a way into the building using ladders and wooden beams as battering rams. As they attacked the front gates they destroyed the revolving door, but though they badly damaged the protective steel doors they couldn't breach them.

When the demonstrators eventually did manage to force the entry gates and gain access to the ground floor, the fighting centered on the stairway leading to the mezzanine. *Telegraaf* employees had barricaded the stairwell with desks and other office furniture. They fought the rioters with chairs, iron bars, and fire extinguishers. They rolled out fire hoses and washed a few of their attackers down the stairs. They succeeded in driving the construction workers back from the stairwell and other points in the building. At 11:20 A.M. several demonstrators entered the building of the *Trouw (Trust)*, a newspaper next door to the *Telegraaf*. The female employees at *Trouw* were advised to leave the building by a fire escape at the back. The battle lasted 75 minutes. By 11:50 A.M., when the police finally arrived, the demonstrators had disbanded and dispersed.

The story of the interaction between the police and the staff of *De Telegraaf* gives clear indication of just how unprepared Amsterdam's bureaucrats were for an uprising against them. During the fighting, *De Telegraaf*'s senior editorial staff — Brandt, Kuijk and Selman — repeatedly telephoned the police. At 10:40 they were told, "We'll be there in five minutes." Eventually they were advised to phone Mayor Van Hall himself. Brandt got Van Hall on his personal line at 11:00 and told him that some of the demonstrators had entered the building and that the police seemed to be waiting for Van Hall's instructions before taking any action. Brandt requested immediate assistance. Van Hall replied that *De Telegraaf* would have to hold off its 100 attackers (the number that Brandt had given him), because elsewhere in the city 1,500 demonstrators were massed. When Brandt replied that the 100 demonstrators attacking *De Telegraaf* were a more immediate threat than 1,500 others "massed elsewhere," Van Hall responded that he was in an important meeting at the moment addressing just this problem. It was not until 11:20 A.M. that Commissioner Molenkamp informed Brandt that the Mobile Unit would be deployed, and it was another twenty minutes before they arrived.

The *Telegraaf* building sustained extensive damage. Windows on the lower levels were shattered and the floor of the director's office on the second story was littered with bricks. The entire building was dripping with water, which on the lower floors had mixed with printers' ink. The street in front was littered with burnt overturned vehicles, damaged automobiles, and half-burned stacks of *De Telegraaf*.

At police headquarters Commissioner Molenkamp and other top officials were powerless to do anything as long as Van der Molen remained in conference with Van Hall. Molenkamp tried to keep Van der Molen informed by means of notes: he phoned the Stadhuis, where J. A. Mittelmeijer wrote down his messages and urgent questions and passed them to Hoogenboom, who was in the conference room with Van Hall and Van der Molen. Rather than giving them directly to Van der Molen, Hoogenboom passed the notes to his superior, Mayor Van Hall. This bizarre situation, where Van Hall spoke on the phone for more than an hour with the staff of *De Telegraaf*, members of the Amsterdam judiciary, and the Ministers of the Interior and Justice in The Hague, yet restricted contact with Van der Molen, the one man who might have had some immediate effect on events, has never been adequately explained.

After calling Mittelmeijer a fourth time and waiting ten minutes for a reply, Molenkamp remembered the direct line to Van Hall's office in the Police Chief's office. It was 11:15 A.M. when he finally managed to speak in person to Van Hall. He asked permission to deploy the Mobile Unit, which was equipped with carbines and tear gas. Van Hall quickly passed the telephone to Van der Molen, who immediately granted the request. Molenkamp later testified that it was only then that he realized that Van Hall and Van der Molen were already aware of the situation at *De Telegraaf*.

It is still not known exactly what was discussed at the conference at the Stadhuis during the 75 minutes when *De Telegraaf* was under siege. Present at that meeting were Van Hall, Van der Molen, Gelinck (the Attorney-General for the province of North Holland), Van den Berg (the Municipal Secretary), and Hoogenboom. Their later testimony before the parliamentary investigative committee was vague and contradictory and the notes on which Molenkamp's frantic messages were recorded had disappeared. It is a monumental irony that *De Telegraaf*, the Netherlands' loudest voice for law-and-order, should have been let down so badly by its own cherished police force in its hour of greatest need.

the midday battle

Since the demonstrators had dispersed before the Mobile Unit arrived, the police drove from *De Telegraaf* to the Stadhuis, which was quiet, and then on in the direction of the Dam. By then the crowd that had attacked *De Telegraaf* was leaving the Dam in the direction of the Central Railway Station by way of the Damrak. The demonstration had grown from a few hundred construction workers to include a wide cross-section of the city's population. As it headed towards the Dam, the Mobile Unit found itself confronted by a mob swollen by office workers on their lunch break, foreign tourists, and supporters of Provo. The police, who were not yet at full force or equipped with anti-riot gear, were unable to take effective action.

In an action typical of Provo tactics, one group of demonstrators unrolled an enormous roll of paper they had taken from *De Telegraaf* while another set fire to its tail as it trailed down the Damrak. The mixture of police, construction workers, Provos and their supporters, and the general public was resulting in chaos. Public sentiment began to turn against the confused police, who were bent on controlling a demonstration and became indiscriminately violent toward everyone. The rioters continually dispersed and regrouped. Whenever the police advanced toward the Central Station the Damrak filled up behind them, with the demonstrators at their backs throwing stones, bottles, and whatever else they could find.

The testimony of Floris Schaper, the most seriously wounded victim of the June 14th riots, lends a living, personal reality to the confusing details of the day. Schaper was a 32-year-old nonunion construction worker at the time. Though he was not an activist, he was one of the crowd of 5,000 at the Dokwerker Monument that morning. He had gone to work at 7:00 A.M. to find his co-workers engaged in a heated discussion about the events of the previous evening. Moments later a mob of between 400 and 500 construction workers arrived and persuaded Schaper and his friends to join the demonstration at the Dokwerker. Schaper said he was too far away to hear the speakers but did witness a group of men chase a policeman, who was rescued by other members in the crowd.

Afterwards Schaper followed the group bound for *De Telegraaf*, where he watched the action from across the street. And when that action was over he followed the demonstrators across the Dam and down the Damrak. For a while he was caught up in the spirit of the events, shouting "Thieves! Murderers!" along with the rest of the crowd. But he soon tired of that, and since there would be no work that day he decided to visit his mother-in-law, who lived nearby. Just as Schaper left the Damrak the first members of the Mobile Unit moved towards the demonstration. He paused to watch the demonstrators arm themselves with bottles and stones to battle the police. A nearby truck was loaded with 7-Up bottles, both filled and empty — an excellent source of ammunition. Schaper stated that when he saw the bottles flying over his head he thought he had better leave and headed up the Oudebrugsteeg, a narrow street that runs off the Damrak.

As Schaper left the demonstration a police motorcycle equipped with a sidecar and carrying two officers headed down the Oudebrugsteeg. The crowd dragged one of the officers from the motorcycle and beat him up. The other officer drew his pistol and threatened to shoot, but his warning was ignored. He aimed his weapon at the leg of the nearest attacker then ducked to avoid a man swinging an iron chair at him from a nearby restaurant terrace. Several shots rang out. The man with the chair was hit in the arm and Schaper, who was halfway down the alley, was shot in the back. The bullet grazed his right kidney, passed through his liver, and exited his body. He crawled away. People in the stores along the narrow street dared not open their doors to help him. Before too long he was discovered by members of the Mobile Unit who had come to rescue their beleaguered colleagues. A shopkeeper phoned for an ambulance and Schaper was taken to the hospital in critical condition. Only days later did it become clear that he would eventually make a full recovery.

Initially, Schaper was believed to have attacked the police with the iron chair and it was reported that way in the press. But the suggestion that he might have been partly at fault was less important than the fact that news of the shooting spread rapidly through the city, inflaming rumors of three more deaths. The shooting moved rioters to reconsider the situation. Many of the striking workers returned to their homes, but the nozems, whom Van Duyn has called the "Monster of Amsterdam," took to the streets.

At 1:00 P.M. a delegation of construction workers met with Van Hall to discuss the 2% cut in vacation pay. Unfortunately, the Mayor was powerless to act. The decision for the pay cut had been made by the unions at the national level. The delegation called for a general meeting at the Dokwerker Monument at 3:30 and tried to persuade Van Hall to speak to the workers, now returning to the streets, but he declined. At the meeting the delegation reported on their conversation with the Mayor to the assembled workers, who were furious when they learned that nothing could be done. They broke the remaining windows in the nearby office of the *Sociaal Fonds voor de Bouwnijverheid*. Though Klaas Staphorst proposed a wait-and-see attitude, the workers were impatient. Some of them stoned a van full of military police, who fought them off. By 4:00 P.M. the construction workers had returned to the Damrak and were prepared for more rioting.

Most of the national government in The Hague was basically unaware of what was happening in Amsterdam. But the Ministers of the Interior and Justice were kept informed of events by their subordinates in Amsterdam and decided to visit the city that same afternoon to view the situation at first hand. The two ministers chastised Van Hall for failing to send the police to *De Telegraaf* in a timely manner. They also decided to reinforce the Amsterdam police with several hundred national and military police.

In the Netherlands the government is nationally centralized. Both the Police Chief and the Mayor were appointed by The Hague. The Ministers of the Interior and Justice were dissatisfied with Mayor Van Hall's leadership of the police and planned to relieve both him and Van der Molen of their duties. They met with Van Hall at the Amsterdam Stadhuis. A number of high-ranking officials were present at the meeting and Van Hall was asked to account for the absence of the police at *De Telegraaf* while it was under siege earlier in the day. He replied that there were not enough police available to handle the situation and that government officials in The Hague had made it difficult for the city to request reinforcements. Though both claims were disputed, the Mayor managed to retain his position until May 1967, when the Commission for Research into the Amsterdam Riots published its report. The report took exception to Van Hall's inaction.

While the two ministers met with Van Hall, the riots continued in full swing on the Damrak. Windows were broken in two large department stores near the Dam. Tacks were strewn across the Damrak, resulting in many police vehicles with flat tires. The Damrak was littered with demolished parking meters, felled traffic signs, garbage cans, and broken glass from automobile windows and storefronts. As soon as the Sanitation Department cleared the piles of debris, bands of rioters streamed in and renewed them. Soon the Rokin, the wide street below the Damrak, was littered with debris as well, as were the narrow side streets in back of the *Beurs* (Stock Exchange), off the Damrak. Then, quite abruptly, at 6:00 P.M. both sides in this strange Dutch Civil War broke away to sit down to their evening meal. Public traffic temporarily resumed on the Damrak. Although the traffic lights had been destroyed, by 6:45 the streetcars were running again.

the battle ends

The sunset on June 14th was lovely, but by 7:15 P.M. the Mobile Unit stationed at the Dam informed police headquarters that the square was crowded again. The rioters had returned from dinner. At 8:00 the streetcars came to a halt once more. Molenkamp kept the offices of *De Telegraaf* under guard through the night, but the building was ignored by the demonstrators. By 8:30 the fight was concentrated on the Dam. Nozems were tearing up cobblestones to throw at the police. Construction huts were turned into barricades. The police battled demonstrators for the rest of the night. Fortunately, though injuries piled up on both sides of the battle line, no one else was shot.

Spokespersons for the Communist Party and Provo Irene Donner-van der Wetering condemned the riots, for which both the communists and Provo were being blamed. Communist taxi drivers, unaware of the Party's position, organized a procession of cabs that blasted their horns as they drove through the city. The streets became choked with burning automobiles and roofing-company tar wagons. Gangs of youth ran back and forth through the narrow streets, with the police in hot pursuit. Someone drove around a truck full of stones for use as ammunition by the rioters. In all, seven foreign tourists from Germany and Japan were injured by flying glass at the entrance of the hotel *Die Port Van Cleve* when police charged a barricade that rioters had erected in front of the hotel. By late that evening several hundred national and military police reinforcements had arrived on the scene.

The warm weather held for two more days, during which time the riots gradually came to a halt. There were 15 arrests on Wednesday, and three on Thursday. Jan Weggelaar was buried at noon on Friday. His funeral was conducted in an orderly manner, and that night it rained. The center of Amsterdam was almost completely deserted. The Battle of Amsterdam had come to an end.

the provo perspective

On June 14th, while the Communist Party and the workers at the Dokwerker collected money for Jan Weggelaar's widow, the Provos had participated in a sit-down strike on the streetcar tracks that crossed the Dam as part of a protest against police brutality. Writing of the violent demonstration on the Nieuwe Zijds Voorburgwal, Van Duyn claims that *De Telegraaf* served the demonstrators as a scapegoat for the absent police, enabling them to vent their anger at Weggelaar's death. He compares the attack on *De Telegraaf* in 1966 to the attack on the Dutch Communist newspaper *De Waarheid (The Truth)* during the Hungarian uprising in 1956, the difference being that the earlier attack had the blessing and tolerance of the government whereas the latter was an act of revolt against the state. He comments that the nozems who participated in the three days of fighting did so out of a craving for some first-hand experience of adventure in their lives, and reports that whole families trekked to Amsterdam from other cities in order to experience a riot. In spite of overwhelming popular support to continue the strike, Van Duyn writes that the Communist-controlled strike committee voted to end it. The Communists did their best to keep the workers from rioting but had little success. It was, in short, a completely popular uprising fueled by a frustration that no authority could control.

According to Van Duyn, the Provos were in sympathy with the attack on *De Telegraaf*, but didn't support the subsequent rioting later that day and on the succeeding nights of the 15th and the 16th. However, it is unlikely that he is an acceptable spokesperson for all the Provos when he says that the ongoing rioting detracted public focus from the real issues of the day: police brutality and the 2% cut in vacation pay. It is true that the riots gave the national government an excuse for unleashing even more police upon the city of Amsterdam. It is also clearly true that the "Provotariat" was a force to be reckoned with in the Netherlands, converging as it did from all points of the country. Indeed the Amsterdam nozems were only a small part of the overall rioting contingent. Van Duyn is clear sighted when he concludes that the Provotariat was only the tip of the iceberg of discontent in the Netherlands, and that the Provo movement had no control over the actions of the young rioters.

On June 14th, the dramatic political momentum of the Provo movement came to an end, although another 7 or 8 weeks would elapse before the tumult that Provo had generated over the past year finally wound down. Through the rest of the summer of 1966, Provo crawled slowly toward the consummation of its destiny.

works referenced

Anarchy (1966) #66 (vol. 6, #8); Duyn (1967); Fahrenfort, Janszen, and Sanders (1966).

8. aftermath of the battle: the gradual decline and death of provo (june 15, 1966–may 14, 1967)

It is far simpler to chart the gestation and birth of Provo than to untangle the threads of its gradual demise, fitfully chronicled in the Dutch press through late 1966 and early 1967. Nevertheless, to understand why Provo died, why its magic failed, we must follow the movement's last eleven months. Van Duyn wrote his important book, *Het witte gevaar (The White Danger)* in November of 1966. He views the timeframe that followed in the wake of the June 14th riots as a period of inertia in which all demonstrations were doomed to become repetitive and anti-climactic. The Happenings, demonstrations, and arrests continued, but they failed to break new ground. The Provos were unable to generate any effective and innovative new imagery, they couldn't reshape oppressive authority in a form that both enraged the nozem Monster of Amsterdam and engaged the working population of the city, and they failed to outline a new trajectory of provocation. Even Robert Jasper Grootveld, who returned to Amsterdam from Italy in August, two months after the riots, could not come up with a novel perspective. Van Duyn says simply, "We aimed too short."

The post-riot tensions didn't cool off immediately. Two major forces still opposed one another. The anti-Vietnam War peace movement continued filling the city's streets with demonstrations for another month, stirring political passions and continuing the fight between protesters and police. Provo activity continued through the summer and autumn of 1966 with particular focus on demonstrations protesting the war, though by that time other groups had taken leadership of the peace movement. In its survey of the period from June 23rd to July 10th 1966, *Elsevier's Weekblad* noted that the police and national military police arrested 295 people in 18 days. The charges included disturbing the peace, failure to disperse, and participation in a prohibited demonstration against the Vietnam War. Most of those arrested belonged to seven youth groups, including Provo, *Rode Jeugd* (Red Youth), the Students Union, and

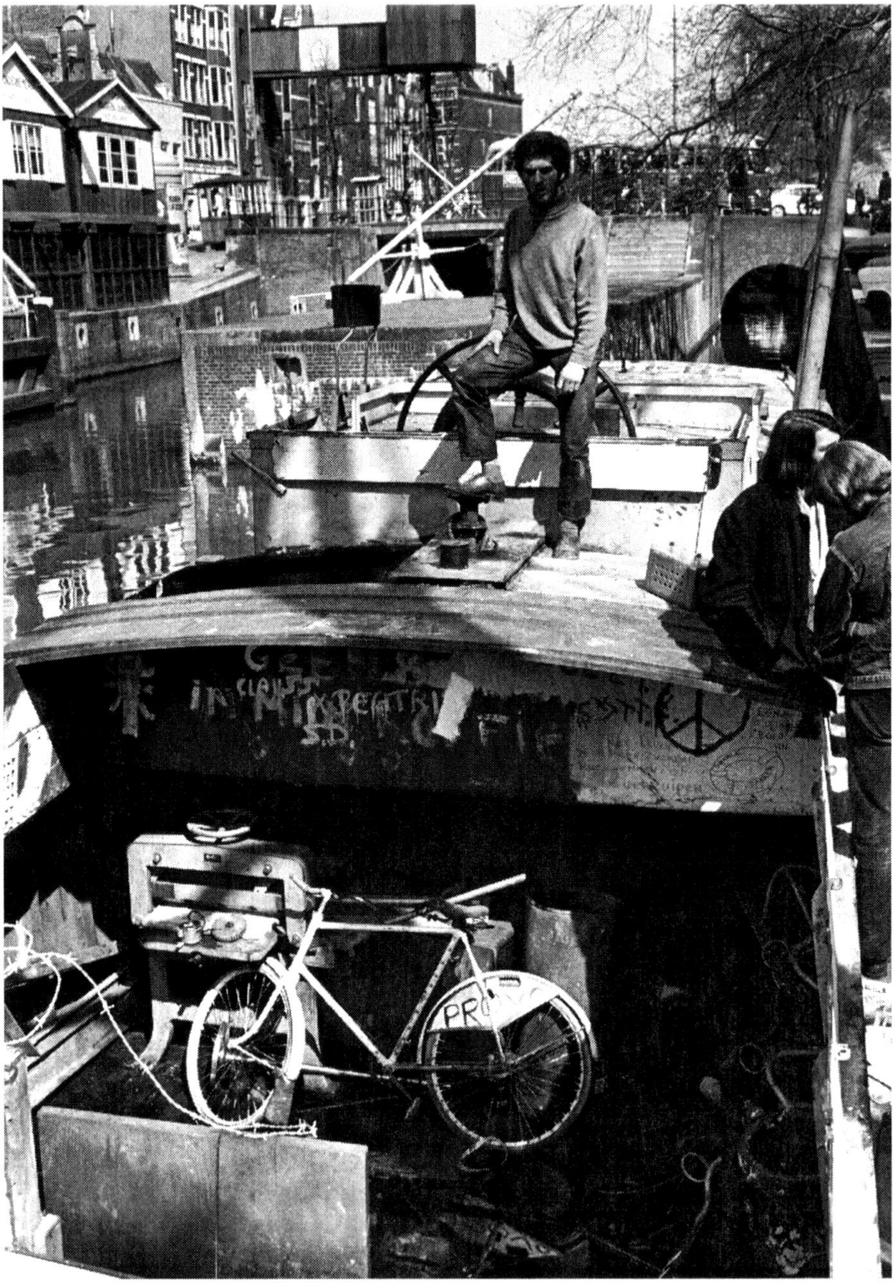

De Witte Neger (The White Negro), the Provo boat. Note the White Bicycle on board the boat.

Aktiegroep Vietnam (Vietnam Action Group).

Yelling "Johnson Mordenaar!" (Johnson Murderer) at a demonstration led to immediate arrest for insulting a friendly chief-of-state, a criminal offense in the Netherlands according to an extension of the Dutch law of *lese-majeste*. This archaic law, enforced only in the Netherlands, would soon be repealed, but in the Provo spirit of play demonstrators easily subverted it by yelling "Johnson *Molenaar*!" (Johnson Miller) instead. Legally speaking this was inoffensive, and Molenaar, as they shouted it, sounded remarkably like Mordenaar.

Some reports from this period claim that police violence had subsided. However, by mid-November 1966 some 28 complaints of police brutality in Amsterdam were making their way through the channels of the Ministry of Justice. Some of these charges were brought by innocent bystanders who had been severely injured by unjustified police attacks. Nevertheless, Provo could generate neither publicity nor solid active response from the ongoing situation.

Hans Tuynman published his book his book *Full-Time Provo* and used the proceeds from the sales to purchase a houseboat in the winter of 1966. This became the short-lived and notorious Provo boat, "Hashiminh" (the name was apparently coined from the words Hashish and the last part of Ho-Chi-Minh, the Communist leader of North Vietnam, demonstrating yet another instance of Provo's fondness for wordplay). The boat was burned in April 1967 by nozems from the Central Station area who had grown jealous because the Provos were getting more attention and state money than they were. Rather than retaliate, the Provos offered the nozems the shared use of their Provo cinema on the nearby Haarlemmerstraat.

One immediate result of the Battle for Amsterdam was that the authority figures that Provo had targeted began to fall. Police Chief Van der Molen was fired on July 16th, 1966. Both the right-wing press and the Provos speculated openly that he was being made a scapegoat for the ineptitude of Mayor Van Hall's municipal government, which proved true. Van Hall and Van der Molen were on the worst of terms and Van Hall's critics eventually learned that the Police Chief had been stripped of any real power before the riots. When the Enschede Commission (*Commissie voor Onderzoek Amsterdam*) published its three-volume report on the June 14th riots, one result was the firing of the "arch-villain" Gijsbert van Hall. He was removed on May 12th, 1967, just two days before Provo declared itself dead at a meeting in Amsterdam's Vondelpark. Provo outlasted its declared major foe by only two days.

The two ministers of the national government in The Hague most concerned with the June 14th riots and the Provo movement fared quite differently from one another. Three days after the June 14th riots, Jan Smallenbroek, the Minister of Justice, failed to report hitting a parked car while driving down the street where he lived in The Hague, making him a hit-and-run driver. He was quickly traced from testimony by his neighbors and was eventually forced to resign his post in the government. On August 1, Ivo Samkalden, the Minister of the Interior, was appointed the next Mayor of Amsterdam.

These two ministers, who had led the government attack on the Provos, were themselves under attack by *De Telegraaf* for leaning too far to the left. The conservative paper was not pleased with the Socialist-Catholic coalition government of Prime Minister Cals, one of the most liberal governments the Netherlands had ever seen. *De Telegraaf* launched a vindictive attack on Smallenbroek after his hit-and-run accident and it seems delightfully ironic that the man who chewed out Gijsbert Van Hall behind closed doors and pressured for the Mayor's immediate dismissal had to resign from office himself at the end of August. Another aspect of the overall ironic tableau lies in the conservative role played by the Dutch Communist Party throughout the Provo period. The Provos weren't fighting "evil men," they were fighting an outmoded authoritarian outlook maintained by a different generation of "good people." In fact, many observers hardly considered Provo to be within the Dutch political spectrum at all. And Provo, battling as it was against all authoritarian mentality, banished the other Dutch political parties from serious consideration in the spectrum of its own political thought.

indefinite note towards a conclusion

The narrative of Provo's political success essentially ends with the June 14th riots in 1966. In 1965, against a background of lethargic apathy, Provo had set itself in isolated opposition to both the Monarchy and the Dutch government's tacit support of the war in Vietnam and Portuguese colonialism as a member of NATO. Provo had endorsed Robert Jasper Grootveld's declaration of war against consumerism, and, to put it in a nutshell, had challenged all authoritarianism in the Netherlands. By virtue of a chance-in-a-million pun that manifested Grootveld's prophesied apocalyptic Santa Claus in the person of an ex-Nazi named Claus Von Amsberg, and by the brilliant tactics of creative PROVOcation, Provo had brought Amsterdam to the brink of social revolution. But the spontaneous revolution failed, just as it was to fail in France two years later.

Though the press, the government, and even the Provos didn't know it at the time, the movement had lost its momentum. It continued to function only on the inertia of its own myth and in response to the pressing issues of the day. As long as the momentum held, anything might have happened. Provo was creating and being created by history, but its trajectory was so unprecedented as to seem outside of both history and political theory. However, once the momentum snapped, Provo became subject to harsh criticism and analysis.

Many of Provo's tactical moves have been questioned. Should Provo have participated in the Amsterdam municipal elections? Was Provo too reformist? Should the Provos have eschewed the student movement? Should Provo have tied itself more closely to the working class? These are important critiques and questions. But though Provo may have failed to theoretically define the larger issues of what a movement and a revolution ultimately are, it is wise to recall that social laws and theories are themselves subject to modification by the events of ongoing history. Thus, leaving the shape of revolution undefined became its own sort of tactic — one opposed to the traditional Communist position that denies the possibility of a "spontaneous revolution," insisting that only its own theoretical formulation of ideological cadres and membership in the Party can successfully execute a revolution. There may be some truth in claiming that anarchism has never adequately addressed the problems inherent in spontaneous revolution, for unlike Communism it has consistently refused to institutionalize the notion of revolution. But that is also likely one of its strengths.

As many social theorists have noted, the moment of truth for a social movement comes when it must institutionalize or face dispersion. Ernst Troeltsch's classic study *The Social Teachings of the Christian Church*, written in German in 1911 and translated into English in 1931, traces the development of the Apostolic sect of Jesus until it becomes the Roman church of Paul, demonstrating at length the development of religious movements or sects into churches, religious institutions. The charismatic figure of the prophet is replaced by the official eminence of the pope and the College of Cardinals — a process described by Max Weber, a German contemporary of Troeltsch, as the routinization of charisma. The plotting, underground communalist ascetic gives way to the crafty, overfed bureaucrat, and "magic" is transformed into ritual and routine. Even the United States, let it be recalled, began as a revolutionary movement. Institutions tend to ossify as revolutionary ardor cools and becomes commemorated in holidays, history, and shrines with just lip service rendered to the shadow memory of revolution.

After June 14th, Provo faced reorganization as a political party, a political journal, or possibly a cult or a discussion group. Instead the Provos chose a symbolic death, much like the funeral procession held by the hippies of Haight-Ashbury in October of 1967. They were conscious of the institutionalizing factor and chose not to "become old news." Abetted by their anarchist outlook and a ludic distaste for the drudgery of everyday politics they deliberately chose the path of dissolution. Inspiration had gone out of the movement so it became time to close shop.

the provo concilium, borgharen, november 1966

The Provo Concilium, modeled in name and vaguely in concept on Vatican II, met on the weekend of November 12th, 1966 in Borgharen Castle on the outskirts of Maastricht, capital of the Dutch province of Limburg. Although billed as international, those in attendance came almost entirely from the Netherlands and Belgium. The meeting began outside the castle on Saturday with a ritual washing of the feet after which fifty participants, interlaced with unraveled toilet paper and yelling "Communication," entered the building. Roel van Duyn made the opening speech, and that evening Robert Jasper Grootveld spoke on "Creative Economics and the Klaasbank" which was a system of economic barter to replace money. At midnight, after the press had left, a procession of twenty people with their heads wrapped in silver foil followed a girl carrying a burning torch and sang "Johnson is een mordenaar." But the police made no arrests.

On Sunday morning Rob Stolk and several of his associates arrived waving a red flag in the name of the RTR, the *Revolutionaire Terroristische Raad* (Revolutionary Terrorist Council). They declared the Concilium to be illegal and claimed to have overthrown the Concilium leadership. (They had already seized the Provo press in Amsterdam and moved it to a hidden location.) After several hours of heated debate, chaired by Luud Schimmelpenninck who wielded a broom as a gavel, the attendees passed several unanimous resolutions.

Among the resolutions passed were:

> The intention to publish secret documents exposing Prince Bernhard's role in the Bilderberg Conferences, annual meetings that were held by government leaders, military chiefs, and industrialists of various countries;
>
> The initial formulation of anti-NATO provocations under the slogan S.O.S., *De SHAPE Op het Schavot* (SHAPE On the Gallows). (SHAPE was the military command of West European NATO forces and was headquartered in Brussels.);
>
> A resolution to send Provo delegations to both North and South Vietnam in order to gather information on the situation there;

A plan for demonstrations protesting the deaths of five anarchists in Spain;

Plans for anti-tourist and anti-advertising activities;

A resolution to establish an international Provo magazine that would publish selections of the best revolutionary articles from all over Europe.

(A decision to stage a second Concilium never came to pass.)

Despite these hopeful resolutions, Borgharen was the first definite sign of Provo's demise. The conference failed in its aim at internationalizing and exporting the Provo movement, and the conference programs and the resolutions that were unanimously adopted failed to take fire. The unmistakable evidence of a split in the original nuclear ranks of Provo had become obvious, something far more significant than simple personality conflicts.

Early in 1967, possibly in January or February, Aad Van der Mijn conducted an interview with Rob Stolk that was published in *De Gids*, a prestigious Dutch cultural magazine. It was entitled "*Provo na de dood van Provo*" ("Provo After the Death of Provo"), and is particularly valuable as little else has ever been published either by or about Stolk. The winter interim of 1966–1967 was proving to be a fatal period of inactivity, and the movement was coming to a complete standstill. The interview sharply underlines the mood of the period. Provo was probing the reason and need for its continued existence, wondering whether it should continue to exist, and what role it should properly play.

Van der Mijn mentions that there have been few Happenings, provocations, or pamphlets in recent months, and notes that *Provo #13* was making a tardy appearance after an unduly long silence. He asks if Provo is, indeed, dead. Listing the movement's "assets," he notes that there are perhaps twenty-five active members with a cellar, a boat, two printing presses, and a closed-down movie house at their disposal, all of which had been bought with the proceeds of the sale of *Provo*, but adding that *Provo* has a debt of 8,000 guilders (about $2,000 US).

When asked if the Provo movement might continue, or if it has anywhere to go, Stolk replied that its past power had resided in its mystique. For the present moment all he could hope for were a few small victories, adding that Provo was never more than that. Stolk no longer felt that any radical improvement in society was possible as long as the masses remained unaware of their own destiny. When Van der Mijn asked if such a realization was a long way off, Stolk replied that people continued to go to their jobs and allow themselves to be exploited, brainwashed by television and advertising. He reiterated his point that change wasn't possible as long as the masses let themselves be led.

When asked if Provo was in a slump, Stolk characterized the June 14th riots as a case of mass hysteria that had nothing to do with Provo. According to him, the movement had never held hope for the arrival of "The Great Revolution." Yes, Provo now had plans, but Stolk didn't see the need for a member on the City Council, because a sign in a demonstration could accomplish just as much as an elected official. He stated that democracy was a semi-fascist dictatorship whose existence makes opposition a necessity. He felt that people might again turn to violence, just as they had during the June 14th riots, because essentially nothing had changed. He himself didn't believe in violence, but he could understand why people reacted violently.

Stolk said that Provo was a small group of people who met regularly in a cellar, a group kept together by the collective memory of an event that had passed its prime. The appeal of the movement had passed, and Provo was probably no longer of any significance to its following, the Provotariat. He noted that Provo was continually changing, that there were new groups following their own version of "Provo." People who had never done anything before were learning about printing, typing, and photography. Should Provo disappear they would probably fall back on their old ways, but Stolk felt that resistance would continue, even if it took on a violent aspect. Provo had been beaten down on everything they tried to do. Resistance would continue because "the street Provotariat feels itself to be the Vietcong of Amsterdam. They shoot at anything that is American."

In an interview conducted by J. Van Tijn, a political journalist for the left-leaning weekly *Vrij Nederland (Free Netherlands)* and published on March 4, 1967, Luud Schimmelpenninck, who was the current representative for Provo on the City Council, agreed with much that Rob Stolk had to say. Schimmelpenninck echoed the observation that confrontation with the police would continue, even as he found it positive that Provo had given the Provotariat something to believe in and fight for. He felt that *Provo*, the magazine, was more important than the seat on the City Council, but thought the movement needed to find a new message. Possibly *Provo* could develop into a political journal. The Provo movement, according to Schimmelpenninck, had been a pacesetter, participating in the first demonstration against the Vietnam War. He also felt that something along the lines of Robert Jasper Grootveld's present project of adopting Americans as a race of loveable idiots might signal a novel approach for a new movement trajectory.

At this point in time Grootveld had moved to Copenhagen,

Denmark, where he was busily preparing his new theory. Of this new theory Schimmelpenninck said that it was characteristically Provo, in that it was an idea that no one else had thought of before. He mentioned that in Amsterdam demonstrators against the Vietnam War were passing out chewing gum, echoing Lyndon Johnson's visit to the Netherlands as Vice-President just a few weeks before President Kennedy was assassinated. (On the occasion of that visit Johnson had passed out chewing gum, a blatantly American commodity, to Dutch crowds. The gesture was widely commented upon in the Dutch press.)

In their interviews, both Stolk and Schimmelpenninck seemed to hold out some hope for Provo's future. But the hope was faint. The actual ceremonial death of the Provo movement occurred on May 15th, 1967 at the Speaker's Corner in the Vondelpark. The Vondelpark is Amsterdam's mile-long park near the city center named for the 17th-century playwright Joost van den Vondel, the "Dutch Shakespeare." It is a favorite gathering place for Amsterdammers. As *Vrij Nederland* described the ceremony, "several hundred Provos, journalists, photographers, members of parliament, plain-clothes policemen, and Harry Mulisch" assembled for the late afternoon event. A number of people made speeches. Among them was Roel Van Duyn, who called for the movement to continue its operation under a different name. Rob Stolk, on the other hand, said that in light of the disappearance of so many who had made it great, Provo no longer had a reason to exist: Mayor Van Hall had been fired two days earlier, Police Chief Van der Molen was gone, and the Minister of Justice Jan Smallenbroek had been forced to resign. Hans Tuynman called for the continuation of illegal activity. Jaap Ham, a rank-and-file Provo, vociferously opposed the dissolution of Provo. He earned his living selling *Provo* magazine and cried, "The bread has been stolen right out of our mouths." Many favored continuing some of the Provo activities, particularly the magazine, the boat, and the movie house.

A decision needed to be made about Luud Schimmelpenninck's seat on the City Council. One suggestion was to sell the seat to D-66, a new left-of-center party. However, a member of the crowd protested loudly that Provo owed something to the 13,000 people who had voted them into office. So the assembly agreed to let Schimmelpenninck continue in office so his White Bicycle Plan could be presented to the City Council. After that the meeting disintegrated, with the crowd moving on to the Lieverdje to sing "friendly songs" to the police, who gladly obliged it by breaking up the final Provo assembly — the Lieverdje had become a forbidden zone.

legacy

Unpredictability was the watermark of the Provo movement, and so long as matters stayed unpredictable the police were unable to successfully contain it. So long as they were unpredictable, the Provos could count on the adhesion of a sizeable public following. They could capture and mirror the collective unconscious of a considerable part of the Amsterdam populace. So it seems possible that by entering the municipal elections in June 1966 they committed a fatal error; they made themselves predictable. They gave up the elements of suspense and surprise that constituted their main weapons of attack and counterattack.

In Jean-Paul Sartre's analysis, a "Fused Group" (or revolutionary mob) can be viewed as an unpredictable moment in history, a moment that can only be prophesized but not predicted (see Appendix 7). It is only in becoming predictable that the Fused Group loses its momentum, by becoming an organization. Though it seems true that on one level human beings crave predictability and organization, and at certain moments of revolutionary chaos they often choose to accept rules and organization out of fear of the chaos their revolution has engendered, by studying the chaos of the unpredictable Provo moment we may come to understand something of the tension of revolutionary creativity: why it cannot, or why it should, be prolonged — the golden possibility of an alchemy of dialectical Time.

The Provo movement owed its successful momentum to a series of fortuitous incidents, but to one incident in particular. Had Princess Beatrix married a German nobleman named Heinrich or Friedrich or Wolfgang, instead of Claus, the phenomenal magical energy ring of Robert Jasper Grootveld's Sabbath-night incantations would never have found circuit completion and release in electrifying charge. Whether by Magic or Destiny, Grootveld uttered the prophetic word *Klaas*, which became the fulcrum for an ominous teeter-totter that very nearly tipped the whole Kingdom of the Netherlands into an apocalypse and could have unseated the Monarchy.

And if magic and destiny weren't playing a role, then Beatrix certainly flaunted history when she chose to marry an ex-German soldier and still maintain her right of succession to the throne. It was odd that the Princess chose to marry that German and no other. Claus was 13 years her senior, and so was barely old enough to be drafted as a Nazi soldier. Had she married a German closer to her own age, or one whose parents had an anti-fascist record there would have been little ground for the public outrage that nourished the newborn Provo movement. And had her sister, Princess Irene, not married a Spanish fascist only the year before there might not have been such a bitter outcry against the royal family in general. But all these oddities did coalesce as history and magic and destiny conspired to give the Netherlands a considerable jolt in 1965.

But one last alchemical reaction was required to transmute the magic energy of Robert Jasper Grootveld's incantation. That agent was the Dutch government, and its catalyst was Provo. Had there not been such harsh repression against the demonstrations opposing the marriage, there would have been no explosion in 1966. Had the politicians held the royal wedding in The Hague or at the Royal Palace of Queen Juliana in Soestdijk, there would have been little or no storm to ruffle the calm surface of Dutch life. But the Crown Princess and the Dutch government willed it otherwise. They defied the Grachtengordel, the magically endowed canal belt of central Amsterdam, and so the Monster of Amsterdam raised its head (and its fist) and the enigmatically smiling and diminutive statue of the Lieverdje became the magnetic center of the fleeting, Illegal Republic of the Netherlands — Shadow Anarchist Republic of the Spirit.

works referenced

"Borgharen," in *Vrij Nederland* (Nov. 19, 1966); "De dood van Provo" (The Death of Provo), in *Vrij Nederland* (May 20, 1967), p. 20; Duyn (1967); "Happenings, Perpetuum Mobile," in *Elseviers Weekblad* (July 16, 1966); *POR* #3 (1967); Sartre (1976); Tijn (1967), p. 7; Troeltsch (1931); Van den Berg (1967); Van der Mijn (1967), pp. 134–136.

appendix 1: new babylon

New Babylon was the utopian vision first conceived in 1956 by the Dutch artist Constant Nieuwenhuys (born 1920, died 2006) and eagerly adopted by the Provos, with his blessings, as their own. Constant is generally referred to by his first name. In 1947 Constant became a founding member of the COBRA abstract painters group, for which he was an important spokesman (see Chapter 1). He left COBRA in 1951 and resigned from the influential Paris-based Internationale Situationiste, an ultra-left artists group, in 1960. He became identified with the Provo movement as it developed and was an important contributor to *Provo* magazine and a candidate on the Provo list for the Amsterdam City Council.

Constant's utopia was imagined for a population that would come into being some 50–100 years after 1965. Its citizens would pass their time in perpetual tourism living in hotel-like accommodations clustered every so many miles across the face of the Earth on platforms of 25–50 hectares (about 55–110 acres) raised 16 meters (50 feet) from the ground. The rest of the Earth's surface would be given over to agriculture, nature preserves, and historic buildings and monuments. (The whole concept has caused many commentators to shudder, foreseeing in its perpetual tourism only an unsatisfying, mandatory, eternal youth-hostelling.)

Constant's utopia furnished the Provos with the battle cry "New Babylon!", which they used in their ecological white plans to campaign for a better and more livable Amsterdam and a better quality of life in general. It also gave them a model that contrasted sharply with the capitalist system and furnished them with a radical socio-economic critique of society on a utopian plane.

Roel Van Duyn was especially enthusiastic about Constant's vision of New Babylon: a cybernetic paradise in which total automation of the means of production would bring about total welfare and a socialist-anarchist state in which authorities would be superfluous. People would be freed from work because labor would be done by computers and robots. "Living-time" would replace "work-time," and free time and creativity would be optimally developed. Humankind would be delivered from the drudgery of work to become the "Homo Ludens," the playing man (a concept developed by the Dutch historian Johan Huizinga in a different context).

In a long article entitled "New Babylon" that appeared in *Provo* and was subsequently anthologized in *Het slechtste uit* Provo (*The worst from* Provo — so titled as to avoid a lawsuit from the Dutch edition of *The Best From the Reader's Digest*), Constant sketched his classically technocratic utopia at length. Automated factories would be built underground in order to avoid pollution. Some human workers would still be needed because not all labor can be automated, but humankind would be collectively liberated from work and free to engage in creativity. Human potential lay in developing creativity, which Constant felt would be possible under such a new economy. He stressed the fact that the technological development of the '60s made his vision feasible.

"Use" would be replaced by "Play" once people were freed of the necessity of work. They would be free to roam the face of the Earth. Fixed residence would be replaced by temporary accommodation. Transportation would become joy riding — Constant thought that the Provos' White Bicycle Plan would evolve into a "White Helicopter Plan." He characterized Robert Jasper Grootveld's Anti-Smoking Temple as an exemplary "anti-functional space," a place where function no longer reigned but was replaced by play and the pursuit of "useless activity." Constant viewed the Provo Happenings at the Lieverdje as an enactment of his vision of New Babylon on a miniature scale.

It was his belief that automation would destabilize capitalism by throwing many workers out of work and, further, that socialism in the Communist nations was better able to handle the phenomenon of automation than was Western capitalism.

appendix 2: provo and the situationists

It is often difficult to know exactly how much one radical movement interacts with another, but in the case of the Situationists and Provo there is clear evidence that they shared certain antecedents and an ongoing "contact with the elements of the radical base." In the years immediately preceding 1968, the Situationists under the direction of Guy Debord were making careful efforts to differentiate themselves and their specific theoretical contributions from all others. Since the Situationist International had purged Constant from its ranks in 1960, when Provo declared itself defunct in 1967 the editors of the *Internationale Situationniste* couldn't resist commenting.

Revolt and Recuperation in Holland
Internationale Situationniste #11 (October 1967)

The celebrated and ephemeral "Provo" movement has often been linked to the SI [Situationist International]. There were the revelations contained in a widely read article published in *Figaro Litteraire* (4/8/1966) — "Behind the angry young men of Amsterdam we find an Occult International" — and the equally popular article in the Belgian journal *Syntheses*, published in April [1967], which took into account the "radical argumentation" that the SI opposes to the derisory sub-ludic moderatism of the Provo "intellectuals," and contained our prediction that the Provo movement was about to end, which was something it did not fail to in May [1967], when it dissolved. While it is quite true that "the Provos have invented nothing," it is, however, quite wrong to suppose that "the Provos provide the previously isolated theorists of the Situationist International with troops, 'intelligent surrogates,' capable of constituting the secular arm of an organization which itself prefers to remain more or less behind the scenes" (*Figaro Litteraire*). We don't consider ourselves so isolated that we need to keep such company; and it goes without saying that we don't want any sort of "troops," even if they were much better troops than these. Indeed, the relationship between the SI and the Provos occurred elsewhere, on two distinct planes. As a spontaneous expression of the revolt appearing in European youth, the Provos usually positioned themselves on the terrain defined by situationist critique (against capitalist abundance, in favor of a fusion of art and everyday life, etc.). Furthermore, as they fell under the influence of a directorship composed of "philosophers" and suspect artists, they encountered people who were also somewhat acquainted with the SI's theses. But this dissimulated knowledge was at the same time the simple recuperated falsification of various fragments. It is sufficient to note the presence in the Provo hierarchy of the ex-Situationist Constant, with whom we broke in 1960. Back then, Constant's technocratic tendencies prevented him from seeing things from the perspective of a revolution that he deemed to be "nonexistent" (cf., *I.S. #3*). As soon as the Provo movement became fashionable, Constant rediscovered revolution, and he slipped in, under the name "anarchist urbanism," the eternal maquettes of "his" unitary urbanism, exhibited at that very moment at the Venice Biennale under the original title so that he would make a good impression. Constant represented Holland as its official artist. The rout of the Provos was already inscribed in their submission to an internal hierarchy and in the idiotic ideology that they devised so that their hastily organized hierarchy could function. The SI has only ever had contact with the elements of the radical base, which should be distinguished from the official movement; and we have always advocated an urgent split from the latter.

We do not want to take the trouble here of returning once more to such a dull theoretical subject: sufficient critique of the doctrine and behavior of the Provos has already been made in the English journal *Heatwave* [cf. Franklin Rosemont and Charles Radcliffe, *Dancin' in the Streets!*, pp. 417–24], and in our brochure *On the Poverty of Student Life* [cf. Ken Knabb, *Situationist International Anthology*, pp. 327–28]. But it is above all the practical development of the contradictions of contemporary society that, having created the authentic element of the Provo revolt, has carried out its derisory institutionalization. The greatest demonstrations of the Provo's conformism were their regurgitation of the sociologico-journalistic dogma that holds that the proletariat has disappeared and their certainty that the workers are now satisfied and perfectly bourgeoisified. The riot that began in Amsterdam on 14 June 1966 and continued for the next few days, the extent of which cast the Provos in the falsest of lights, showed that their movement was in reality already dead. The Provo movement was indeed dead that June day, because this was *an exemplary workers' riot* of our era, one that began as an attack upon the bureaucratic union building, continued as a battle with the police (and the reinforcements who came from their supporters in the harbor district), and culminated as an attempt to destroy the office-block occupied by that great daily newspaper, *The Telegraaf*, because it of course published false news. Indeed, most of the rebellious youth of Amsterdam (for it would be false to identify all the Provos as a student movement) joined the workers in the street. But the Provo hierarchy, upon discovering in the conflict the negation of its piteous ideology, was faithful only to itself: it disavowed the violence, condemned the workers, appealed for calm on radio and television, and promoted other banalities before spectacularly leaving town en masse, in order to provide a good example of passivity.

If the Situationists certainly anticipated the Provos in regard to a few vague novelties, there is all the same a central point we flatter ourselves on, which is the fact that we relentlessly remain "nineteenth century." History is still young; and the proletarian project of a classless society, even if it began badly, is still more of a radically new curiosity than the achievements of molecular chemistry and astrophysics put together or the billions of fabricated events channeled by the spectacle. Despite our "avant-gardism" and *thanks to it*, it is only to this movement that we want to return.

[Translation by Reuben Keehan, online at http://www.notbored.org/provos.html]

appendix 3: dada influences

In 1916, at the height of World War I's brutality, Dada emerged from a nightclub called *Cabaret Voltaire* in Zurich, Switzerland, when a group of expatriate artists organized a series of outrageous and provocative anti-cultural manifestations that served as a desperate total protest. The Dadaists were protesting both the senseless war that had engulfed them and the obsolete art forms of European civilization.

The history of Dadaism is well known (see Hans Richter's *Dada, Art, and Anti-Art*, for one version). It had a tremendous influence on almost every form of modern art. It might even be said that Dada supplied the alphabet for much of the innovative artistic language of the Western world at mid-century. En route it gave rise to the Surrealist movement and it still appeared as fresh as the day it was conceived when it resurfaced amidst receptive artists and intellectuals in the 1950s. Among the art forms it influenced were theater of the absurd, sound poetry, concrete poetry, performance art, collage, Happenings, and mixed media in general. Dadaism imparted a strong sense of playful irony to every movement it touched. The Dada manifestos from 1916 through the 1920s find their echo in the social sentiments of many 1960s Anarchist movements, Provo among them. Dada was totally, even ruthlessly, anti-authoritarian. The freedom of the individual was highly prized. From this perspective it can be seen as the artistic corollary of political Anarchism.

A campaign leaflet that Roel Van Duyn wrote for the City Council elections insisted that Provo was a rare historical phenomenon comparable (in his words) "to the teachings of Socrates, the invention of printing, Halley's comet, or Dadaism." Though later admitting that he may have been bombastic, nevertheless he continued to assert that at least the comparison with Dadaism was historically defensible. The Dadaists had used terms such as *provocation* and *to provoke* so frequently that Van Duyn voiced surprise that they had not come up with the term *Provo* themselves. Significantly, he dedicates the 5th chapter in his book *Het witte gevaar* (*The White Danger*) to a history of Dadaism, including generous quotes from Hulsenbeck, Hugo Ball, Tristan Tzara, Hans (Jean) Arp, Raoul Haussmann, and Theo Van Doesburg.

By far the most obvious Provo sympathizer of Dadaism is Robert Jasper Grootveld. Grootveld's performance activities vividly recall performance strategies exploited by the Berlin Dadaist Johannes Baader, the self-proclaimed "Ober-Dada" (Supreme Dada) of the early 1920s.

According to Van Duyn, Baader was a prophetic monomaniac who proclaimed himself Jesus Christ returned to Earth. He wrote letters to the Kaiser and to the French government, and was arrested at the outbreak of World War I as a danger to the State. In 1917 he was an unsuccessful candidate for parliament, and in 1919 he broke up a meeting of the parliament in Weimar when he threw copies of one of his pamphlets over the heads of the astonished legislators, an incident that made headlines in the German press. In the pamphlet, which was entitled *Das Grune Leiche* (*The Green Corpse*), he asked the German people if they were willing to give the Ober-Dada a free hand. He promised to bring them Order, Peace, Freedom, and Bread — in November 1918 he had caused an uproar in the Lutheran Cathedral in Berlin when he yelled out in the midst of the service that Jesus Christ was a sausage. (Pandemonium broke out and charges of blasphemy were brought against him.)

There is also a correlation between the language of Grootveld's manifestos and the language used by the Dutch Dadaist Theo Van Doesburg. Van Doesburg is best remembered as the founder of "De Stijl" group. De Stijl was a Dutch version of Bauhaus. Its best-known figure is Piet Mondriaan, noted for his beautiful primary-color paintings of black-edged rectangles in red, blue, yellow, and white. Van Doesburg painted, designed interiors, and did architectural work. At the same time, with the assistance of the German Dadaist Kurt Schwitters (who was not considered "Dada" by many of the German Dadaists), he tirelessly attempted to introduce Dadaism into the Netherlands. He and Schwitters toured the country giving a series of riotous performances during which Schwitters barked like a dog to substitute for his lack of knowledge of the Dutch language. (See Robert Motherwell's *Dada Painters and Poets* for a delightful account of two of these evenings.) Van Doesburg also smuggled Dadaist poetry into the pages of *De Stijl*, the movement's magazine under the pseudonyms of I. K. Bonset and Aldo Camini.

With regard to Provo and Grootveld, Van Doesburg's most important text seems to be the fourteen-page manifesto "Wat is Dada?" Van Doesburg's language there seems to prefigure that of the manifestos that Grootveld delivered at the K. Temple and the Lieverdje, and the manifestos Simon Vinkenoog produced for some of the happenings. Van Duyn devotes a page of *Het witte gevaar* to quotes from "Wat is Dada?"

In his manifesto, Van Doesburg put forth a version of Dada that did not believe in the spiritual content of life, art, religion, philosophy, or politics, but insisted that they instead relied solely on publicity and the power of suggestion. People let themselves be manipulated by symbols that were repeated so often that they left an indelible impression: religion was represented by the Cross, Nietzsche by his thick mustache, Oscar Wilde by his homosexuality, and so on. Dada realizes, Van Doesburg declared, that through experience anyone can win over the masses as long as one appeals to their atavistic instincts through powerful well-publicized suggestions.

According to Van Doesburg, Dada views every dogma or formula as a stopgap measure designed to keep afloat the sinking ship of Western civilization. Noting the fraud that sustains every aspect of civilization, Dada declares the world bankrupt. As presented by Van Doesburg, Dada was the international expression of collective experience over the ten years preceding his manifesto, a reaction to the wanton destructiveness of World War I. Dada is "the most immediate expression of our formless times. . . . Dada does not have any aspirations for immortality. . . . Dada has always existed but was only discovered in our times."

Based on these stylistic similarities and person connections, it is clear that Dadaism was one model for action that influenced Robert Jasper Grootveld; it was a model masterfully transmuted by this "Smoke Magician" and his Provo associates to affect the spirit of Amsterdam in the Sixties.

works referenced

Baljeu (1974); Van Duyn (1967); Motherwell (1951); Richter (1965); Schippers (1974)

appendix 4: anarchist antecedents in amsterdam

The anarchist tradition, often obscured by the more dominant Marxism, was attractive to the new spirit of the Sixties because of its anti-authoritarian stance. Anarchism has its own pantheon of greats: including Proudhon, Kropotkin, and Bakunin, as well as Thoreau, Tolstoy, the Diggers of 17th-century England, the Anarchists of Spain, Oscar Wilde, Sacco & Vanzetti, Gandhi, and several political groups from the Sixties, including the Provos and the Enragés of Paris '68.

In popular thought, anarchism is synonymous with chaos as a figurative term and is visually equated with the image of wild-eyed bomb throwers as a political stance. However, a dispassionate analysis of the history of anarchism would show that politically it should be equated with cooperativism. Anarchy as a political theory stands opposed to the concept of the State; indeed to any authoritarian power structure whatever. The New England town meeting and the positions taken by the later Count Tolstoy or Gandhi would be closer to the anarchist ideal than either the Weathermen of the late 1960s or the numerous assassins of the late 19th and early 20th centuries, who fit the popular stereotype. Rudolf de Jong, a Dutch anarchist historian, wrote that anarchism is anti-Messianic, in that man must liberate himself from any authority, domination or prejudice, and not rely on a Redeemer, a Party, a group, or any other individual. Indeed, the later Diggers of the Haight-Ashbury hippie scene in San Francisco serve as a good American example of anarchism.

One confusion that arises about anarchism is due to the fact that there are at least two major strains of the movement: the cooperativist one, best represented by Kropotkin, and the individualist-terrorist one represented by Stirner and Bakunin. The two Russians, Kropotkin and Bakunin, were the major anarchists of the late 19th century, both of whom lived in exile in Western Europe. Stirner was a German and is slightly more obscure historically. In the United States, the American anarchist tradition was largely forgotten by

1965 and was not a banner that people easily recognized, as was the case in Europe. In the Netherlands it was quite different, and in Amsterdam even more so.

Amsterdam has a rich anarchist tradition that extends almost 100 years before 1965, so the philosophy was no stranger to the city as a viable ideological orientation. It was possible for the Provo youth to be self-consciously anarchist, aware as they were of their city's history. Robert Jasper Grootveld's father was an anarchist and Grootveld, Stolk, and Van Duyn might be called initiators of Dutch neo-Dadaist anarchism.

Amsterdam had three great popular revolts that never faded entirely from popular memory. First was the *Palingoproer* (Eel riots) of 1886, which grew out of an attempt by the police to ban the popular bare-handed eel fishing contest waged by men standing unsupported on boats in the canals of the Jordaan quarter. Van Duyn makes the inescapable comparison between police suppression of the Lieverdje Happenings in 1965 and police actions during the *Palingoproer*. The *Palingoproer* was, on the face of it, a spontaneous non-political uprising, but it was rooted in the terrible poverty of the Jordaan at that time coupled with bitter popular hatred of the police.

In 1917, the *Aardappelrelletjes* (Potato Riots) erupted after the neutral Dutch government made a handsome profit exporting potatoes to both Britain and Germany during World War I at the expense of the poor people of Amsterdam, whose staple food was potatoes (recall Vincent Van Gogh's painting "The Potato Eaters"). Again fighting broke out in the Jordaan quarter and quickly spread throughout the city. Ten people were killed and 114 wounded, but the riots succeeded in putting a stop to the export of potatoes.

In 1934, in the midst of the Depression, there was a spontaneous revolt against the reduction in welfare payments. Once again the revolt began in the Jordaan and spread swiftly to the other working class districts of Amsterdam, as well as to other Dutch cities. In Amsterdam barricades were thrown up in the streets and for six days the workers held out against the government in protest directed at both hunger and the police. Van Duyn calls these revolts "anarchistic" rather than "Anarchist" because there was no consciously anarchist group involved.

The great "classical" anarchist leader in the Netherlands at the turn of the 20th century was Ferdinand Domela Nieuwenhuis (1846–1919), who is still referred to by his middle name. He was, in sharp contrast to anarchist theory, a strongly messianic figure greatly revered in his own lifetime and still widely honored at present. Although there were a great number of anarchist groups and personalities in the Netherlands at this time, Domela's charismatic career has tended to overshadow other anarchist figures in popular memory. He began as a Lutheran minister, but soon changed vocation and published a newspaper, *Recht voor Allen (Justice for All)*, in 1879. In 1886, he was held accountable for the *Palingoproer* and arrested that same year for lese majeste when he wrote that the king "does not pay much attention to his job." He was imprisoned for seven months in 1887, until widespread protests finally set him free. He later helped form the Social Democratic League in the Netherlands and became its first member in parliament. However, he soon grew disgusted with parliamentary socialism and eventually became an anarchist.

The great railroad strike of 1903 almost brought the country to the verge of an anarchistic revolution, with Domela Nieuwenhuis among its many leaders. Unfortunately, at a critical moment the Socialists broke with the striking workers, and the government was able to crush the developing revolt. Domela was worshipped almost as a saint from his own day to 1969 — when students at the University of Amsterdam seized the Maagdehuis (Administration Building) they renamed the university Domela Nieuwenhuis University.

A number of interesting anarchist movements developed in the Netherlands after Domela's death in 1919. One of them had a newspaper, *De Moker: opruiend blad voor jonge arbeiders (The Sledgehammer: Inflammatory Newspaper for Young Workers)*, published in the 1920s. In their manifesto they state that although they are few in number, they will crush each segment of the chain of capitalism "with a sledgehammer in our fist. We shall pulverize everything: the State and the factories, and the entire organization of this society that is based on crime and lack of character. We have been fooled for 2,000 years by Love and Meekness. We shall incite people to hate, to vengeance, and to destruction!"

Another group was the I.A.M.V., the *Internationale Anti-Militaristische Vereniging* (International Anti-War Association) (1904–1940) which Van Duyn considers the most successful Dutch anarchist organization. Its international name notwithstanding, the I.A.M.V. was an entirely Dutch organization. It was not avowedly anarchist but pacifist — though anarchists made up the majority of the membership — and campaigned against people volunteering for military service while advocating independence for the Dutch East Indies (now Indonesia). One of their campaign tactics was strikingly similar to Grootveld's pre-Provo "kanker" campaign. The I.A.M.V. pasted skulls on the recruiting posters of the *Indisch Leger* (Dutch East Indies Army), showing a happy soldier cycling in the tropical sun with the word "Handgeld" (spending money) running across the poster, which they pasted over with the word *Bloedgeld* (blood money).

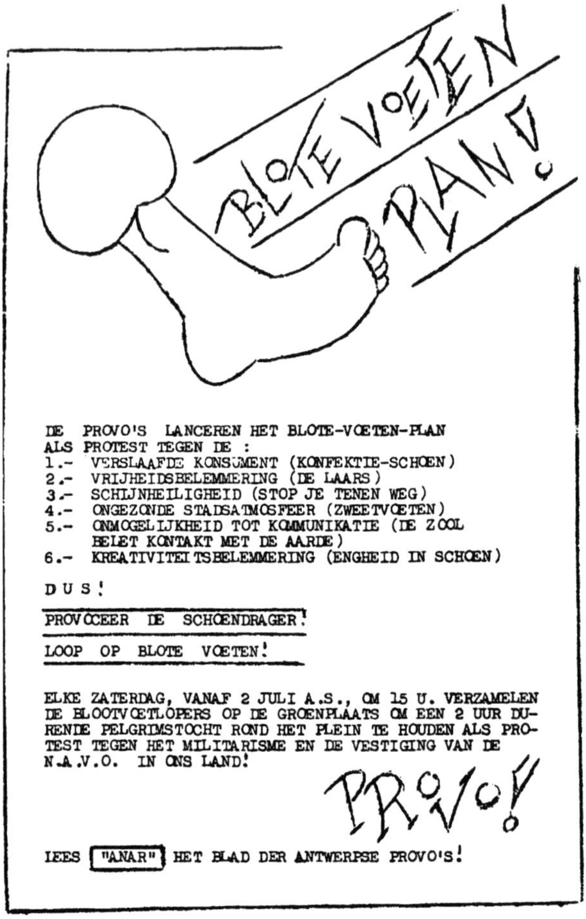
BLOTE VOETEN PLAN!

DE PROVO'S LANCEREN HET BLOTE-VOETEN-PLAN
ALS PROTEST TEGEN DE :
1.- VERSLAAFDE KONSUMENT (KONFEKTIE-SCHOEN)
2.- VRIJHEIDSBELEMMERING (DE LAARS)
3.- SCHIJNHEILIGHEID (STOP JE TENEN WEG)
4.- ONGEZONDE STADSATMOSFEER (ZWEETVOETEN)
5.- ONMOGELIJKHEID TOT KOMMUNIKATIE (DE ZOOL BELET KONTAKT MET DE AARDE)
6.- KREATIVITEITSBELEMMERING (ENGHEID IN SCHOEN)

DUS!

PROVOCEER DE SCHOENDRAGER!

LOOP OP BLOTE VOETEN!

ELKE ZATERDAG, VANAF 2 JULI A.S., OM 15 U. VERZAMELEN DE BLOOTVOETLOPERS OP DE GROENPLAATS OM EEN 2 UUR DURENDE PELGRIMSTOCHT ROND HET PLEIN TE HOUDEN ALS PROTEST TEGEN HET MILITARISME EN DE VESTIGING VAN DE N.A.V.O. IN ONS LAND!

PROVO!

LEES "ANAR" HET BLAD DER ANTWERPSE PROVO'S!

The Bare Feet Plan street theatre flyer.

Translation: The Provos are launching the Bare Feet Plan as a protest against:

1. The addicted consumer (mass-produced shoes)
2. Suppression of freedom (the boot)
3. Hypocricy (hide your toes)
4. Unhealthy city atmosphere (smelly feet)
5. The impossibility of communicating (the shoe sole prevents contact with the earth)
6. Stifling of creativity (tight-fitting shoes)

Therefore: Provoke shoe-wearers! Walk Barefooted! Every Saturday, starting July 2 at 3 pm, barefoot walkers will gather at the Groenplaats to hold a two-hour walk round the square in protest against militarism and the presence of NATO in our country.
Read 'ANAR', the newspaper of the Antwerp Provos!

appendix 5: provos in belgium and the provinces

Amsterdam was the birthplace and metropolis of Provo and remained the location of its heart and head throughout its two year existence, but during the fall of 1965 the movement spread rapidly through Europe's Dutch-speaking regions. It made its presence felt in all large and many smaller cities in both the Netherlands and the Flemish areas of Belgium, including Brussels, the bilingual capital. However, due, I believe, to its isolation in the Dutch language, Provo failed to develop extensively as an international movement. Events simply moved too fast for the necessary translation of its message and thoughts into other languages.

One characteristic common to the various provincial groups was an ersatz Lieverdje: each group organized its Happenings around an appropriate local statue. And almost every fledgling Provo group published a small anarchist "underground" paper, whose name was usually synonymous with that of the local Provo group. The staff that produced the printed paper always served as the nucleus of these loosely organized little groups. Along with Happenings peculiar to its locale, the paper was each group's most distinct manifestation. These little newspapers were always published in Nederlands, called Dutch on one side of the border and Flemish on the other.

The rapid contagion of what the right-wing sensationalist press called the "Lieverdje Sickness" halted instantly at the linguistic frontier, though it easily crossed the Belgian border into Flanders. Belgium is politically and socially a radically different country from the Netherlands and had at that time surprisingly minimal contact with its neighbor to the north. The situation in Brussels illustrates Provo's linguistic isolation quite well. The city had an active Provo group among the Flemish but a French language group failed to materialize — though there were plans to publish *Provo* in French for distribution in Brussels and Paris. Contact with England

and Germany likewise accomplished little. Self-proclaimed Provos did raise their heads in the United States: Los Angeles, Berkeley, and Davis (on University of California campuses), among other places. One legacy of this "invisible" heritage is Provo Park (formerly Constitution Square) across the street from the Berkeley City Hall.

Probably the most interesting and original group in the Dutch provinces was "*Ontbijt Op Bed*" (Breakfast in Bed) in the city of Maastricht, the provincial capital of Dutch Limburg in the extreme southeast corner of the Netherlands. Breakfast in Bed grouped around a magazine of the same name. Van Duyn calls them "the most creative Provo group outside of Amsterdam." He contrasts them with Provo, implying that the tenor of their statements was more violent. The "*Wit Wham-Bom*" (White Wham-Bomb) manifesto, which he quotes at length from *Ontbijt Op Bed #5*, is more sharply edged in its tone than are similar Provo declarations, and its humor is of a darker shade.

"The White-WHAMMM!!!! is the booby trap under God's ass." It would be the bomb under pulpits and altars, under the policeman's cap, under NATO tanks and jets; a bomb in the keel of battleships, under the Dutch throne, and in the beds of corporate presidents. The manifesto calls for the destruction of the homes of the authorities, of churches and automobiles; it calls for destroying Rembrandt's paintings and all "Great Art." "Strike down the concerts of Mozart, the Gregorian chants. Bach is dead, Bach is dead, Bach is dead!!! Crack open the Earth, crumble it up, open an abyss for the presidents and prelates, the flag and the fatherland. Burn, White-WHAMMM!!! Anyone can make a Deluxe-Bomb. Everyone his own white Whammm!!!"

Besides Ontbijt Op Bed there was what Van Duyn calls a second more "orthodox" group in Maastricht that staged Happenings around the local Geis statue beginning in April 1966. Their events were never covered in the local press because of an agreement between the press and the police not to furnish the movement with any publicity. The agreement came to an end when the police took the Geis statue from its pedestal and locked it up. In September 1966, a second Provo magazine, *Lynx*, appeared in Maastricht. *Lynx* had the same name as the Provo paper in The Hague. (The name refers to a wild member of the cat family and was adopted by the Provos as a pun on the Dutch word *links*, meaning Left.) It was more politically oriented than *Ontbijt Op Bed*.

Van Duyn also identifies Provo groups in Utrecht, Leeuwarden, Vaals, Amersfoort, Leiden and Dordrecht, among other Dutch cities. He also notes small groups abroad: in Stockholm, London, Manchester, Oxford, Paris, Milan, Prague (where there were many arrests), New York, Chicago, and Philadelphia.

In Brussels there were two favored sites for Provo activity: the Place de Brouckere at the northern rim of the city center, and the Porte Louise, the "official" southern entry to the city center. Happenings always took place at the same time every week, regardless of the weather — 5:00 P.M. on Saturday afternoon. The police made more than 50 arrests at a dozen Happenings during the period of peak activity, from October 1966 to the end of the year. At one particularly Belgian Happening the Provos hung a white flag bearing the word *Provo* on the steps of the Church of the Peres Carmes. A bale of straw at the foot of the steps of the church was set afire to attract public attention, and a Provo speaker urged the crowd that gathered to demonstrate against the war in Vietnam. The speaker opposed New York Cardinal Spellman's declaration that the American military were "Soldiers of Christ." When the gendarmes (police) arrived, the Provo minding the fire was arrested, as were two others who were passing out leaflets. The speaker fled into the church, where the gendarmes dared not follow. When they did finally enter the church they caused a commotion because they failed to remove their caps — during which the Provo orator quietly slipped out another door. Frustrated, the police arrested a dozen people from the crowd outside the church.

appendix 6: the kabouters (1970)

On June 3rd, 1970, a new Dutch anarchist group attracted international attention when they won five of the 45 seats on the Amsterdam City Council, as well as two seats on the councils in The Hague and Leeuwarden, and one seat on the councils in Arnhem, Alkmaar, and Leiden. The Kabouters (pronounced Kab-Out-Ers, meaning gnomes or leprechauns) were an offshoot of Provo. Their parliamentary "leader" in Amsterdam was Roel Van Duyn, who had successfully defended the single seat originally won by the Provos in 1966.

Van Duyn's turn to occupy the seat for a rotating one-year term, a practice peculiar to the Provos, had finally come in 1969. At the time he took his seat the Provos had been reincarnated, in a fashion, in a group called *Oranje Vrijstaat* (the Orange Free State), a double pun on the royal Dutch House of Orange and the South African Boer Republic of the 19th century. It was the Kabouter name for the "liberated zone" of the new anarchist communes and cooperative businesses that were now operating in the Netherlands. Van Duyn wrote a council memorandum to create the "*Volksuniversiteit voor Sabotage Teknieken*" (Peoples' University for Sabotage Techniques).

One objective of the Kabouter group, which had been founded in January 1970, was to set up an alternative society based on ideas outlined in Van Duyn's recently published book, *De boodschap van een wijze Kabouter (The Message of a Wise Kabouter)*. In an article discussing the new philosophical position, the *Krant van Oranje Vrijstaat Arnhem (Newspaper for the Orange Free State of Arnhem)* wrote that Van Duyn's struggles as a Provo had been based on despair, but that he had changed after reading the work of Peter Kropotkin. The article identifies the Provo movement as "Bakunist," based on terror and violence, and the Kabouters as "Cooperativist," based on the work of Kropotkin.

The Kabouters were most visible in Amsterdam, but had an active membership in about thirty-five Dutch cities. At the peak of the movement's activity, around June 1970, about 500 people attended the weekly open meetings where plans and policies were discussed. A year later membership had dwindled to 20 people.

The Amsterdam group published 12 issues of the *Kabouterkrant (Kabouter Newspaper)* in 1970. *Kabouterkrant* concentrated on information about meetings and local Amsterdam activities rather than discussing political ideas, historical background, or current issues such as Vietnam and Angola, as had been the case with *Provo* magazine. There was little discussion of broader issues. Indeed, entire issues of the *Kabouterkrant* make no mention of international affairs. Physically the paper was more "professionally" designed. It appeared in tabloid format numbering about 12 pages per issue, with many photographs and a self-conscious layout that sometimes creates a visually "heavy" page full of story headlines. Ink is more evenly distributed than was the case with Provo — every letter of every word is visible. The color of the ink varies with each issue: entire issues came out in purple, olive drab, or brown (issue #9 was printed in black on orange paper, greatly hindering its legibility).

The Kabouters organized themselves into various "departments," which roughly corresponded to government ministries and acted as the shadow government for the alternative society of the Oranje Vrijstaat. The departments included *Bejaardenhulp* (Help for the Elderly), *Cultuur*, *Voedsel* (Food), *Huisvesting* (Housing), *Onderwijs* (Education), *Alternatieve Banen* (Alternative Jobs), and *Sabotage*. Bejaardenhulp was the strongest department and survived the collapse of the Kabouter movement, having existed prior to the movement. The Kabouters were a direct outgrowth of the ecological platform of the Provo White Plans, and featured "*Groenen Planen*" (Green Plans) such as the idea to have plants growing in boxes on top of automobiles and to have the automobiles drive on sunken roadways so that pedestrians would only see a procession of moving greenery. The idea, which seems (characteristically) facetiously provocative, was to bring greenery into the city. Van Duyn actually introduced it as a motion before the City Council.

The Kabouter members of the city councils considered themselves ambassadors to the Netherlands from the Oranje Free State collectives, and viewed themselves as outsiders. The term *klootjesvolk* (testicle folk) which the Provos had used to refer to the silent majority that was satisfied to consume and loved automobiles (see Chapter 4) was replaced with *Trol* (Trolls), the polluting "bad guys." The fairytale and gnomish imagery of the Kabouters irritated some former Provos. Rob Stolk, who at that time was active in the Nieuwemarkt neighborhood activist program in central Amsterdam, felt that the Kabouters were not negative enough in their outlook.

The most significant and lasting Kabouter contribution to direct action politics was introduce the "kraken" tactic: they "cracked" (squatted) empty buildings to create new housing in Amsterdam. The Netherlands has been the most densely populated country in the world for almost five centuries, with the situation aggravated by the high percentage of soggy reclaimed farmland suitable only for agriculture. People often waited years before getting married because they were forced to live with their parents until they could find suitable housing of their own. Therefore the action of "liberating" empty buildings from speculative absentee landlords was supported by Dutch public opinion. The police and municipal officials often (but not always) came down hard on these activities.

According to Van Duyn, the Kabouters fell apart as a movement primarily because of internal dissension. The main issue was whether to participate as a party in the national parliamentary elections, in April 1971. The movement split down the middle on this issue. Many Kabouters felt that the electoral process was not anarchist and consequently they entered the elections divided and failed to place any candidates. The defeat in the national elections collapsed the nationwide movement overnight. There was also disagreement among the five Kabouter members on the Amsterdam City Council. Two of them were strong advocates for the legalization of marijuana and smoked it in chamber sessions. Van Duyn disagreed with their tactic, feeling that the issue was unimportant. The two smokers threw a stink bomb during one City Council meeting, forcing the chamber to adjourn for an hour.

The Kabouter movement incorporated a significant ludic element, particularly among the members from The Hague. During the 1970 municipal election campaign, the twenty-three Kabouter candidates for the council seats in The Hague posed nude for a group portrait in the *Haagse Bos* (Hague Woods) for a campaign poster. This poster was perhaps the most memorable manifestation of the Kabouter ethos. Nudity was a constant feature of The Hague Oranje Vrijstaat. One group staged a witches' play at a national Kabouter picnic in Amersfoort that ended with the cast throwing off its costumes, climaxing (literally) in fornication. (This particular behavior was not common among the national movement as a whole.) For the "*Jericho Actie*" (Jericho Action), several hundred Kabouter supporters marched seven times around Amsterdam's huge new Nederlandse Bank, an unpopular "skyscraper" that had risen in the old city center. Unfortunately, they failed in their attempt to ape Joshua, the Old Testament prophet, and bring down the walls.

Provo was a hard act to follow, but almost everyone involved felt that some attempt had to be made. Robert Jasper Grootveld and several people from the Ontbijt Op Bed anarchists in Maastricht set up an offbeat group called Delta in 1968. Rob Stolk became an activist in the Amsterdam working class district of the Nieuwemarkt.

The Kabouters were the best-known of the subsequent groups, but only Van Duyn, Luud Schimmelpenninck, Hans Tuynman, and a few other original Provos participated in the Kabouter movement.

The marvelous Provo sense of punning was almost totally absent from the Kabouters' political language. Kabouter ideas were more mundane and their sense of humor more anodyne. Their scope of operation and thought was limited to local issues, which circumscribed their political horizon. But perhaps the main problem for the movement was its homogeneity: young middle-class anarchists. The Kabouters sorely needed a "magician" like Robert Jasper Grootveld to facilitate a fruitful fusion with other groups. The nozems, or equally provocative equivalents, were lacking. The Kabouter emphasis was more political than aesthetic, and in the political arena the student groups tended to be hostile to them, leaning instead towards the Dutch Communist Party. To many Dutch people, the Kabouters seemed to be reformed flower children playing at social work.

In all fairness to the Kabouters, however, it must be said that they did make an impressive showing: 40,000 Amsterdammers voted for them in June 1970, and they appeared serious in their attempt to set up an alternative citywide communal society. They coordinated many unaffiliated alternative groups and operated many stores, alternative clothing factories, farms, and other economic and social endeavors that bore fruit. Their newspapers and activities compare favorably with what was happening in the United States at the time. Perhaps the idea of setting up an alternative social system within the confines of any already existing society, even with the best intentions, is doomed to failure.

appendix 7: sartre's concept of the fused group (analytical applications to revolutionary groups of the 1960s)

Jean-Paul Sartre's *Critique of Dialectical Reason*, originally published in French in 1960 and subsequently in English in 1976, is a landmark book of great theoretical potential. Its impact has yet to be fully felt due to Sartre's political independence (which was often viewed as political unreliability), as well as the philosophical opacity of the text. *Critique* is an existentialist re-evaluation of Karl Marx's Marxism — as opposed to the Marxism professed by the various Communist parties of Sartre's day. It is an exercise that attempts to re-contextualize Marxism, simultaneously setting it in philosophical opposition to Kantian analytical thinking, emphasizing anew Marx's close relationship to Hegel, while disavowing what was then labeled "vulgar Marxism" and the polemical (ideological) stances of late party Communism. Sartre's approach re-situated Marxism in the mainstream of Western intellectual thought, removing it from the shallow deterministic 19th-century "scientific" mode adopted by various Communist ideologues. Significantly, his reexamination proves both prescient and insightful when viewed in relation to the political dissidence that emerged during the late-1960s on an international scale, the success of which is perhaps best exemplified by the Provo movement and the May 1968 revolt in France.

Many of the political movements and groupings of the 1960s vindicate Sartre's methodological approach. Many of them consciously applied the term "anarchist" to themselves and the political practices they advocated. *Critique* offers an intelligible model explaining what did and did not happen within the various movements of the 1960s. It also provides an analytical tool that may help future revolutionaries modify their courses of action.

the provos and the french revolt of may 1968

Despite predictable differences stemming from their varied cultural and national backgrounds, the movements that surfaced in the Sixties tend to show similar structural affinities. Taking Provo actions in Amsterdam and the French revolt of 1968 as examples, the shared characteristics can be described as: spontaneity, rejection of what Sartre calls "the Pledge" (adherence to an institutionalized organizational structure), rejection of the "official" positions of political Marxism, awareness of anarchism's historical traditions, a strong measure of art and humor in their praxis, little expectation of success (though both movements were surprisingly successful), and a capacity to respond intelligently to the swift rush of events as they developed. Many similar characteristics were also present in the peace movement in the United States, though they remained diluted there because the workers and the "students" remained polarized. Both Provo and the groups involved in France in '68 faced strong opposition to spontaneous revolt from official union hierarchies, and from the influential Communist parties in their respective countries. And both, through an unexpected alliance of youth and labor, brought their nation-states close to the brink of a civil war, providing a momentary glimpse of the impossible dream of total revolution. The Dutch and French examples set up a typology of revolt, which Sartre's analysis of the "Fused Group" can help explain.

In his book *Existential Marxism in Postwar France: From Sartre to Althusser*, Mark Poster traces the events of May 1968. "For a brief moment, France tasted life beyond alienation," he writes. French people began to talk to one another, tapping the creative potential that their previous isolation had kept dormant. The passive daily existence of meaningless work and consumption "gave way to an exhilarating, joyous festival." Poster calls the movement that generated and sustained the May Revolt in France a classical Fused Group. The generalized popular response that characterized the success of Provo can be seen in a similar light.

The French revolt precipitated as the result of an unusual tactical ploy by the "March 22nd Movement," an eclectic group originating from Nanterre University in suburban Paris that included the avowed anarchist Daniel Cohn-Bendit. The March 22nd group provoked the authorities at the Sorbonne to call the police onto the "sacred grounds" of the university, a place where traditionally the police never trespassed. As police officers arrested the provocateurs, students who were there as bystanders and witnessed the arrests began battling the police themselves — a reaction similar to the one that had manifested in Amsterdam two years earlier. In Sartrean terms, the student bystanders witnessed the *other* when they saw the police loading their fellow students into police vans. Mark Poster has described the formation of "groups-in-fusion," which took place spontaneously when the students tried to prevent the arrests from taking place, thereby breaking the atomic seriality (individual isolation and lack of social cohesion) present in everyday life. The battle at the Sorbonne on May 3rd, 1968 quickly escalated into a student-worker civil war against French authority.

Poster points out that the French Communist Party denounced the student uprising as a frivolous adventure, much as the Dutch Communist Party had done two years earlier with respect to the Provos. The rebels of the Sixties were far more playful than the grim, old-line Marxists. "If you make a social revolution, do it for fun.... Proletarian revolutions will be festivals, or they will not be, for the life they herald will itself be created in festivity. Play is the ultimate rationality of this festival, living without boredom and enjoying without limitation are the only rules to be recognized," insists Mustapha Khayati's widely distributed 1966 Situationist manifesto *On the poverty of student life*. This same joyful concept existed in the Netherlands, where the title of Johan Huizinga's famous book, *Homo Ludens (Man-at-Play)*, became a battle cry of the Provo movement.

Students formed Action Committees to take over the functioning of the universities and other cultural institutions such as the Odeon Theater in Paris, and younger workers, revolting against their unions, often Communist-dominated, set up Action Committees in their factories and offices, sometimes in joint action with the students. Poster notes that although a strong effort was made to form a central organizing group, it failed through the divisiveness of the various groups. Much the same thing happened in the Netherlands throughout the period 1966–70, both with the Provos and with subsequent anarchist groups. Sartrean and Communist critiques of the French revolt and other Sixties movements cite the refusal to institutionalize as the prime cause for the failure of these revolts. The Communist phraseology insisted that the student groups didn't correctly represent the workers because they lacked meaningful organization and unity, and further, as privileged children of the bourgeoisie, had no grasp of the needs of the working class.

The great battle cry of the May 1968 revolt was *Autogestion* (Workers Control), which seems to have encompassed the students' "notion of free choice of one's destiny in collective action." (Poster, 385) The key in France was seen to be seizing control of the means of production, which has never been an anarchist goal. But worker control would have inevitably become reformist if private ownership of capital were left intact. Later Dutch anarchists, such as the Kabouters, tended to advocate smaller, alternative economic units — communes, "free stores," and cooperative printing shops. And like the French revolutionaries they were isolated, surrounded by a dominant society that failed to collapse in the face of collectivist opposition. In France the non-Communist Left became divided, resulting in a power vacuum that President De Gaulle cleverly occupied to reaffirm his hold on state power.

By understanding Sartre's concepts of the Fused Group (emerging from spontaneous revolt) and the Pledge (here seen as the refusal to institutionalize a party bureaucracy), the Sixties movements become comprehensible. The revolts of the Sixties can be seen to mark the first historically conscious employment of dialectical circularity on a reversible basis — less evident in France than in the Netherlands, where the Provos voted themselves out of existence, or in San Francisco, where the hippies held a funeral service for the Haight-Ashbury district in October 1967.

the fused group and the pledge

Sartre's *Critique of Dialectical Reason* consists primarily of a single volume, entitled *Theory of Practical Ensembles*, which is a phenomenological investigation of various modalities (forms) of social formation. In it he posits that material scarcity has existed throughout human history, so people have banded together in larger or smaller groups to better realize the practical aims of the groups' members. But scarcity has also produced an alienation of people from themselves as they have had to surrender much of their lives to the maintenance of economic sustenance, so another goal of social groups has become the struggle to banish alienation from their ranks. However, within each group an inescapable contradiction unavoidably comes into play, for Sartre maintains that the modality in which alienation is overcome, the "Fused Group," is so unstable (lacking in ontological essence) that it reintroduces alienation in order to maintain itself — though this is always done unwittingly. A spontaneous, rebellious mob has no leadership or direction, therefore something — leadership, consensus, and/or policy — must develop to give cohesiveness to the continuance of the revolt. In other words, rebellious individuals form groups, but there must be some degree of group discipline for the rebellious group to survive.

Whenever a Fused Group does succeed in maintaining itself, what eventually emerges are the group modalities that Sartre calls the "Organization" and the 'Institution." Paradoxically, the Organization and the Institution are antithetical to the concept of the Fused Group at the same time as they provide the practical means of coordinating and realizing the tangible aims of some of its original revolutionary ideas. A Fused Group springs out of the alienated seriality (atomized existence) that is characteristic of most human groupings: Sartre gives the example of people waiting in line at a bus queue in order to be transported to their various places of work. These impersonal gatherings are called "Collectivities" in Sartre's terminology. He considers them the basic type of sociality. Historically (or temporally) Fused Groups do not take precedence over Collectivities; their relationship partaking rather of the nature of a reversible reaction. In the Sartrean dialectic the Fused Group can relapse into a Collectivity, such disintegration being predictable. He does state, however, that "Fused groups constitute themselves as... negations of collectives." (Sartre, 1982: 348)

Sartre seeks "to explain the transition of oppressed classes from the state of being collectives to that of revolutionary group praxis." (Ibid., 349) This transformation occurs when an oppressed Collectivity is pushed to a limit where life is no longer possible under conditions imposed by its oppressors. The members of the oppressed Collectivity identify a situation in which they perceive a common danger to themselves, defining themselves by a common objective (overcoming the threat) that in turn identifies a common praxis (course of action).

Sartre's classic example of the Fused Group, taken from the pages of the French Revolution, occurred when the revolutionary mob from the district of the Faubourg Saint-Antoine in Paris stormed the Bastille prison on July 14th, 1789 under duress of threat from the royal militia. "It [the militia] helped the gathering to perceive its own reality as an organized being." (Ibid., 356) Much the same perception was created on May 3rd, 1968, when the police entered the courtyard of the Sorbonne to arrest Daniel Cohn-Bendit and his colleagues from Nanterre. The student reaction to the police action generated a Fused Group, and, in a very real sense, helped expand the student-worker revolt that was to cripple the French nation. A similar action-reaction had developed two years earlier in Amsterdam when repeated police attacks transformed four dozen young Anarchists and their sympathizers into a national political force.

It is in the dialectical opposition between alienated, serialized individuals and an antagonistic State force that a fusion of people takes place in what Sartre calls an "apocalypse." Indeed, no better term can be found describing how the May 1968 revolt and the Provo movement sprang so spectacularly into existence. "This group, though still unstructured, that is to say, entirely amorphous, is characterized by being the direct opposite of 'alterity' (alienation)," he writes. (Ibid., 357) Since Fused Groups form as a result of a dialectical negation and not as a result of praxis, the repressive arm of the State, the police, can be interpreted as being a principle catalyst in forming revolutions. It's a function they often perform as well or better than the professed programs of dedicated cells of revolutionaries.

Sartre observes that the aim of the Fused Group is usually reformist. He cites a strike of the silk weavers in Lyon who were not combating alienation and exploitation, but were opposing a reduction of their wages. Sartre calls the weavers' aim a restoration of the status quo. But, he claims, their action negated such a restoration because society was no longer the same after the revolt. (It is in this context that one should recall the peace movement in the United States, which opposed an illegal and unconstitutional war being fought in Vietnam. Merely by constituting itself, it profoundly altered the social structure of America.) Both the May Revolt and the Provo movement were stigmatized by the Communist parties of their countries as being reformist.

However, a Fused Group "constantly totalizes itself and disappears either by fragmentation (dispersal) or by ossification (inertia)." (Ibid., 407) In other words, once a mob or group accomplishes the immediate goal on hand, it disintegrates. This tends to be a paradigmatic characteristic of the movements of the Sixties. To counteract the tendency toward disintegration, the members of the group take what Sartre calls the "Pledge," in which individuals subject themselves to the discipline of the group, limiting their personal freedom as a guarantee against dispersal. Thus the members of a spontaneous, hastily formed Fused Group now claim membership in that group. Sartre describes the moment of the Pledge as follows: "When freedom becomes common praxis and grounds the permanence of the group by producing its own inertia through itself and in mediated reciprocity." (Ibid., 419)

The moment in the dialectical historical process that Sartre is describing is important, for here is where almost all the movements of the Sixties balked. They refused to take the Pledge. Historically, revolutionaries find it difficult to surrender their individual personal freedoms to the larger entity of the group, an action that was reaffirmed in the movements of the Sixties. As already noted, the Provos voted themselves out of existence and the hippies of San Francisco held their own funeral. Respectively, they refused to institutionalize or to allow themselves to be exploited as media commodities.

Sartre states that the permanent Fused Group is an impossibility. The Sixties was predicated on just this declared impossibility as a first principle. The result was dispersion. But this dispersion, total as it was, was a negation of the kind of bureaucratization that followed in the wake of the 1917 Bolshevik Revolution. A Soviet-like regime was something that the Sixties movements wished to avoid at any cost. Analytically, Sartre's model of the Fused Group with its inexorable march towards Organization, Institution, and Alienation, seems correct, but it was theoretically unacceptable to the movements of the Sixties as a possible dialectical *modus operandi*.

sartre and the sixties

Sartre's *Critique*, supplying as it does, an excellent analytical tool for the 1960s, and Sartre's generous statement of support for the May 1968 revolt, seemed initially to indicate an attempt at a reconciliation of attitude on Sartre's part. However, it is more likely that this appearance of similarity exists on the level of praxis (practice) rather than of theory. A number of factors confuse the issue. First, Sartre would never, and this was consistent on his part, oppose the action of a Fused Group: he was not one to blow an ideological whistle on a mob attacking the proverbial Bastille. His endorsement of May 1968 was an endorsement of praxis as it occurs within the limits of his conception of the dialectical moment of the Fused Group, but was not an endorsement of the spontaneous rebellion's theorizing. Sartre had spoken of the scarcity of material goods in human society before the onset of affluence in Western society, stating that material need was what drove people into social-economic relationships and determined the nature of human interaction. However, he modified his concept of Need in terms of material scarcity. He wrote, "The consciousness of the intolerable character of the system must therefore no longer be sought in the impossibility of satisfying elementary needs, but... in the consciousness of alienation...." (Sartre, 1974: 125) This important modification in his theory brought him somewhat closer to the outlook of the Sixties. Secondly, during the course of events Sartre and the Sixties movements became part of the international spectrum of the non-Communist Left. Sartre spoke of the irreconcilable differences that existed between the Communist parties and any Fused Group.

In Mark Poster's enthusiasm for May 1968 and for what he terms "Existential Marxism," he tends to push the case for theoretical reconciliation too far, although such an eventuality cannot be completely ruled out. The major practical problem of reconciling the revolutionaries' refusal to take the Pledge, with the beneficial social and political phenomena which "rest" in institutionalization, remains to be solved. It was left unresolved by the various movements of the Sixties, and future movements will need to be more focused on this problem.

Sartre wrote, "This is where the problem lies. We are confronted with reaction, with strong and complex capitalist rule, which has an ample capacity of repression and integration. This demands a counter-organization of the class. The problem is to know how to prevent that counter-organization from deteriorating by becoming an 'institution'." (Sartre, 1974: 130) He adds, "It is undoubtedly true that a theory of the passage to socialism is necessary," (Ibid., 130) but notes: "While I recognize the need of an organization, I must confess that I don't see how the problem which confronts any stabilized structure could be resolved." (Ibid., 132; see also 60–61)

What we have seen thus far is that groups constitute themselves as movements on an ad-hoc basis, designed to solve specific issues or to initiate specific crises, then disband upon the completion of the task. By storming the Olympian pinnacles of early 19th-century philosophy to give us this rich sutra of the *Critique*, with its diamond-sharp logic, Sartre has proved himself something of a Prometheus. The activists of the Sixties in France and the Netherlands, in attempting to reverse an inexorable dialectic, re-enacted the myth of Icarus, who flew too close to the Sun. Until future history proves otherwise, the myth of the reversible Fused Group will remain a myth of Icarus.

appendix 8: some comments on a recent critique of the provos

Relatively little new material was published on the Provos between 1970 and the 1992 appearance of Virginie Mamadouh's important study, *De stad in eigen hand: Provos, Kabouters en Krakers als stedelijk sociale beweging* (Amsterdam: Sua, 1992. The title translates approximately as *Popular Control of City Government: Provos, Kabouters, and Squatters as Urban Social Movements*; or, more literally, *The City in One's Own Hands*). The definitive account of the Kabouter movement is *Louter Kabouter: Kroniek van een beweging, 1969–1974 (Pure Kabouter: Chronicle of a Movement, 1969–1974)* by Coen Tasman (Amsterdam:De Geus-Bablylon, 1996). Most recently, in 2003, Niek Pas, an assistant professor at the Institute of Media Studies at the University of Amsterdam, published his doctoral dissertation as *Imaazje!: De verbeelding van Provo, 1965–1967 (Image!: The Imaging of Provo, 1965–1967)* (Amsterdam: Wereldbibliotheek, 2003).

Unfortunately, Pas' book is a major study, a hefty tome of 463 pages of which 90 pages are footnotes and an additional 18 pages include a bibliography and list of sources. It is maddening that such a thorough work should so consistently belittle Provo and its members on page after page. Given Pas's negative view of Provo it is essential that this first major study not be taken as the definitive work on the movement. In response to it, Coen Tasman, author of *Louter Kabouter*, wrote a long critical review that he published in the Dutch periodical *Buiten de Orde* (Herfst 2003).

Pas' book was written from the point of view of Media Studies, an area that is his present specialty. The word *verbeelding* in the title does not have an exact English equivalent, it means "imaging" as well as "self-promoting, wishful thinking, allowing one's imagination to run away, pipe-dreaming, exaggerating," suggesting that the current "image" of Provo is a myth. Thus the title strikes a sarcastic note, echoing the attitude of the author. Throughout his book Pas comes across as an overbearing skeptic, blind to the creativity and uniqueness of Provo. He focuses on the Provos' relationship to the media. However, in order to proceed with his more specific analysis he provides an historical review of Provo. He bristles with skepticism at what he considers to be the movement's pretensions, giving the impression of being right-wing. But on further reflection his negative outlook seems that of a knee-jerk skeptic, unable to accept the validity of Provo on almost any terms.

Pas, who was born in 1970, has absolutely no awareness of the deep moral commitment that was so much a part of the Sixties outlook, and which was characterized by a lack of self-interest, unlimited generosity, compassion for suffering, the willingness to share with others, deep conviction concerning the social responsibility of the individual, and the need to reach out to fellow human beings, all of which was united with a passionate disavowal of the current capitalist society. Without a grasp of this pervasive altruism one cannot possibly begin to understand the phenomenon of the Sixties.

Certainly, Pas is mistaken in evaluating Provo in terms of present-day values. Furthermore, he gives equal weight to all historical sources, without evaluating their validity or identifying their point of view, employing negative opinions of the Provos as justifiable in every circumstance. One particularly salient instance of this shows in his use of quotes from letters-to-the-editor published in *De Telegraaf*, which in the 1960s was a conservative, rabidly anti-Provo newspaper. Pas appears to take these letters, written by readers who would today feel affinity toward Rush Limbaugh, as valid critiques of the movement.

The Provos were open to many influences, both political and artistic, but Pas tends to argue that all their ideas are derivative, even going so far in his attempt to deflate the wide arc of their creativity as to hint at plagiarism on their part. As one example of his general attitude he writes: "Just as Boersma declared himself as a "gnot-magician" and Stolk presented himself as a printer, Van Duijn took on the pose of someone who could ideologically and historically make Provo legitimate. The media and the public lapped it up. It is difficult to judge just how much Van Duijn believed in his own constructions and ideas, and in what measure his imagery only 'served as a means of stirring up tension.'" (Pas, 140; all quotes from Niek Pas are my translations. The end of the final sentence is a direct quote from Van Duijn.) Further, he dismisses Van Duijn's 1967 book, *Het witte gevaar: Een vademecum voor Provos (The White Danger: A Guide for Provos)*, which gives an account of the movement and its theoretical grounding in Dadaism and anarchism, as "above all an autobiography" (Pas, p. 402, footnote 104).

On page 94 of his book, Pas sketches a simplistically reductionist psychological analysis of Grootveld's *Klaas* program, arguing that he abbreviated the childhood memory of Sinterklaas (Santa Claus) to the short phrase "Klaas komt!" (Claus is coming!). And that rather than choose to play the role of Klaas, he preferred to dress as *Zwarte Piet* (Black Pete), the African servant of Sinterklaas, because Klaas was an external force that Grootveld could never hope to be. Pass ignores the fact that Grootveld had always insisted: "I am not Klaas." Klaas was a figure that Grootveld claimed would come into being dialectically. And, as if it were important to Grootveld's theoretical stances, Pas highlights Grootveld's penchant for cross-dressing.

Grootveld and Van Duijn always stressed that publicity was never an end in itself but rather a means of addressing social and judicial reform. Nevertheless, Pas dismisses the White Plans, the Provos' social programs, as publicity stunts — despite clear evidence that Luud Schimmelpennink worked for many years to implement both the White Bicycle Plan and a Witcar (an electrically powered White Car), and the obvious fact that Irene Donner-Van der Wetering was quite serious about the educational aspects of the White Woman Plan. By dismissing the White Plans, Pas strips the Provos of much of their political and social platform. And by denying Provo its anarchism, its disinterestedness, and its passion he seriously distorts the movement's motivations, presenting them as a bunch of attention-grabbing publicity seekers and scheming careerists, implying a deep cynicism on their part.

Completely ignoring the strong anarchist backgrounds of Grootveld, Stolk, and Van Duijn, and the collective impulse behind the White Plans, Pas contends that Provo displayed a total lack of theory. "As was previously noted, in May 1965 Provo had no theoretical orientation." (Pas, pp. 137–138) He calls Provo a "publicity machine" (Pas, pp. 222–223), seeing every aspect of the Provo project as primarily media directed. He dismisses Grootveld's obvious power as an artist, saying only: "Grootveld's mastery was his ability to get noticed in the media" (Pas, p. 87), a remark that negates his insightful and trenchant social commentary.

In picturing the Provos as a cynical, callous cabal that deliberately set itself up as a mythological entity, Pas not only denies them their human generosity, their creativity, and the seriousness of their political convictions but he completely ignores their individual post-Provo commitments, which were often life-long and entailed the sacrifice of a more materially comfortable lifestyle. Many of the Provos continued the trajectory of their activities long after Provo's demise. Grootveld developed his "*piepschuim*" (polystyrene foam) idea, constructing floating islands which he planted with gardens and set out in the harbor to disrupt commercial traffic, a project he pursued for many years. Schimmelpennink devoted himself to the White Bicycle and White Car plans, the latter of which was half-heartedly taken up by the Amsterdam City Council before languishing for lack of adequate funding. Rob Stolk, who did become a printer, remained a political activist and was instrumental in the Nieuwemarkt battle against the proposed underground metro line in the 1970s. Roel van Duijn was for many years a member of the Amsterdam City Council, first as a Provo, then as a Kabouter, and finally as a member of the PPR (Party of Political Radicals). Much later he became an organic farmer in the east of the Netherlands. In fact, Van Duijn, Tuynman, Schimmelpennink, and marginally Grootveld, all became active in the Kabouter movement. Only Bernhard De Vries, the first Provo member on the Amsterdam City Council, can be said to have become something of a careerist when he gave up his seat on the council to launch a career in Italian films, making five of them in the late Sixties and early Seventies.

Pas claims that his book is a thorough study of the Provos. In many ways it is, though it is certainly not unbiased and it does miss the very important March 19th police attack on the people waiting to view the exhibition on the police brutality of that occurred during the demonstrations against the royal wedding. Despite the book's negativity there is much of value to be found in its profuse detail. It gives an excellent interview-based survey of the family and educational backgrounds of Van Duijn, Stolk, and Grootveld, at the same time as it remains unjustly critical of them. Pas's coverage of the developments in Maastricht and Belgium is far-reaching. The twelve-page bibliography and the ninety pages of footnotes provide a wealth of information. It is to be regretted that such a sizeable book could not better serve its subject. Although Pas asserts that his book is a study of Provo's manipulation of the media, he has put the cart before the horse.

annotated general bibliography

Aarts, Joos. *See Van Provo tot Groenevelt.*

Actie, werkelijkheid en fictie in de kunst van de jaren '60 in Nederland (Action, Reality and Fiction in the Art of the Sixties in the Netherlands). Rotterdam: Museum Boymans Van Beuningen, 1979. Art exhibition catalog with much information on the artistic milieu of the Sixties, including the Provo Happenings.

Alverson, Charles. "The Kabouters Are Coming!: Good Scenes and Bad in the Amsterdam Summer." *Rolling Stone*, Oct. 15, 1970, pp. 29–31.

Anarchy (London) No. 66 (Vol. 6, No. 8) (August 1966). [Special issue on the Provo movement] English critiques of the Provos, written shortly after the June 14th riots. "Day Trip to Amsterdam," by Charles Radcliffe, pp. 237–242, is a charming eyewitness account. The issue also includes short texts by Van Duyn and Constant that were translated into English.

Aniba, J. W. F. "Provo-Amsterdam (1965–1967)" *Spiegel Historiael* 21:9 (Sept 1986) pp. 392–399.

Baljeu, Joost. *Theo van Doesburg*. New York: Macmillan, 1974.

Banning, Johan Petrus Dorothée Van. *Het huwelijk van Hare Koninglijk Hoogheid Prinses Beatrix (The Marriage of Her Royal Highness Princess Beatrix)*. Zaltbommel: Europeese Bibliotheek, 1966.

Berg, J. Van den. *De Anatomie van Nederland*. Vol. 1. Amsterdam: De Bezige Bij, 1967. A useful introduction to constitutional and political structures in the Netherlands.

Boehmer, Konrad. *See* Regtien.

Bogers, Hans, et al. *De psychedelische (r)evolutie: Geschiedenis van en recente ontwikkelingen in het Onderzoek naar veranderde bewustzijnstaten*. Hans Bogers, Stephen Snelders, Hans Plomp, voorwoord Simon Vinkenoog. Amsterdam: Bres, 1994.

"Bogharen." *Vrij Nederland*. Nov. 19, 1966.

Bronkhorst, Huub. *See* G. D.

Buikhuizen, Wouter. *Achtergrond van Nozemgedrag (Background to Delinquent Behavior)*. Assen: Van Gorcum, 1965. The doctoral dissertation on the provocative behavior of teenage delinquents from which the Provos derived their name.

C'est demain la veille: Entretiens avec Michel Foucault [etc.]. Paris: Editions du Seuil, 1973. A collection of interviews, including one with Roel Van Duyn. In French.

"City Council's Beatnick." *Holland Herald*, Vol. 1, #5 (1966), p. 15.

Claeys, Herman J. *Wat is links?: Vraaggesprekken over literair engagement....* Brugge: J. Sonneville, 1966. By the leader of the Brussels Provos. Includes an interview with Roel Van Duyn.

Clay, Mel. "Jerry Rubin (Yippie) Meets the Dutch Kabouters (Radicals)." *Los Angeles Free Press*, Nov. 20, 1979, p. 5.

Commissee voor Onderzoek Amsterdam. Rapport. 's-Gravenhage, 1967. V. 2: Bijlage. The official Dutch government report on the events of the Amsterdam riots, commissioned by the Dutch parliament.

Constant. *See also Anarchy*; Haags Gemeentemuseum; Hendriks; Hummelink; Kennedy; Kleijer; Musée Picasso Antibes; Nieuwenhuys, Constant; Phaff; Schierbeek; Stokvis; and Wigley.

Dalny, Jacques. "Playful Provos." *Atlas*, Vol. 12 (Oct 1966), pp. 25–27. A dyspeptic putdown of the Provos claiming that they got all of their ideas from the Situationiste Internationale.

Davidson, Steef. "Subway Culture in Amsterdam." *Ins and Outs: A Magazine of Awareness* (Amsterdam) #2 (July 1978), pp. 5–12. An excellent article on the Nieuwemarkt resistance to subway construction in the early 1970s. Rob Stolk was active in this neighborhood.

"De dood van Provo." ["The Death of Provo."] *Vrij Nederland*, May 20, 1967, p. 20.

De Jong, Rudolf. "Ferdinand Domela Nieuwenhuis: Anarchist and Messiah." *Delta* (Amsterdam), Vol. 13, No. 4 (Winter 1970–1971), pp. 65–78.

______. "Provos and Kabouters," in *Anarchism Today*, edited by David E. Apter and James Joll. Garden City, N.Y.: Doubleday, 1972. Good chapter in English by a Dutch historian of Anarchism; pp. 191–209.

De Jongh, A. *Provo: een jaar Provo-activiteiten*. Rotterdam: Uitgeverij Kerco, 1966.

De Lobel, Wim. *En toen kwam Provo: Herinneringen aan de jaren zestig*. De As: Anarchistische Tijdschrift 16 (83) (July/Sept 1988), pp. 5–11.

De prinses die kiest een man. [*The Princess Who Chose a Husband*.] Martin Van Amerongen [et al.]. Amsterdam: Polak & Van Gennep, 1965. On Princess Beatrix's courtship and marriage.

De Rooy, Piet. *Een revolutie die voorbij ging: Domela Nieuwenhuis en het Palingoproer*. Bussum: Fibula-Van Dishoeck, 1971.

Delta: A Review of Arts, Life and Thought in the Netherlands, Vol. 10, No. 3 (Autumn 1967). Amsterdam: Delta International Publication Foundation. [Special issue on the Provos] An excellent 152-page survey, in English, of the political aspects of the movement, available in many larger research libraries.

Droge, Philip. *Beroep meesterspion: Het geheime leven van Prins Bernhard*.

Amsterdam: Vassallucci, 2003. An account of Prince Bernhard's Nazi party membership in the 1930s, as well as his involvement in various intelligence agencies for four countries.

Duijn,* Roel Van. *Provo: De geschiedenis van de provotarische beweging, 1965–1967.* [*Provo: The History of the Provotarian Movement.*] Amsterdam: Meulenhoff, 1985. A revision of Van Duyn's Het witte gevaar, with much added information and some omissions, i.e. Dadaism; including numerous photographs of the events by Cor Jaring. *Note that the author has changed the spelling of his name.

Duyn, Roel Van. "Pre-Provo Anarchisme." In *Het slechste uit Provo.* Amsterdam: De Bezige Bij, 1967a, pp. 44–65.

______. *Het slechste uit Provo: een bloemlezing uit alle verschenen nummers van het tijdschrift "Provo"; samengesteld en ingeleid door Roel Van Duyn.* [*The worst of Provo: An Anthology From All the Published Issues of the Magazine "Provo", edited and introduced by Roel Van Duyn.*] Amsterdam: De bezige Bij, 1967b. A selection of articles from all the issues of Provo magazine.

______. *Het witte gevaar: een vademecum voor Provos.* Amsterdam: Meulenhoff, 1967c. This is a major source of information on the Provo movement and the historical antecedents that influenced it written by one of the movement's founders.

______. *Message of a Wise Kabouter.* London: Duckworth, 1972. English translation of De Boodschapen van een wijze Kabouter.

______. *Schuldbetekenis van een ambassadeur: nota's, beschouwingen, manifesten, artikelen en vragen van een ambassadeur van Oranjevrijstaat in de Gemeenteraad van Amsterdam.* [*Guilty Confession of an Ambassador: Notes, Reflections, Manifestos, Articles and Questions of an Ambassador from the Orange Free State to the City Council of Amsterdam.*] Amsterdam: Meulenhof, 1970. Van Duyn's account of his first year on the City Council serving as a member of the Kabouter Party.

Ellemers, J. E. "Nederland in de jaren zestig en zeventig." *Sociologische Gids*, Jrg. 26:6 (nov/dec 1979), pp. 429–451.

______. "The Netherlands in the Sixties and Seventies." *Netherlands Journal of Sociology*, Vol. 17 (1981), pp. 113–135. An English translation of the previous citation.

Elseviers Weekblad (Amsterdam). A conservative Dutch weekly news magazine, closely modeled on Time Magazine; particularly useful for following events in 1966. In the course of covering the Provos and the anti-war movement the magazine gradually moved to a more supportive position.

Fahrenfort, Jacques, Henk Janszen, en Fred Sanders. *Oproer in Amsterdam: Het verhaal van twee historische dagen, 13–14 juni 1966. [Revolt in Amsterdam: The Story of Two Historic Days, June 13th–14th, 1966.]* Amsterdam: Becht, [1966?]. The most detailed account of the June riots in Amsterdam; written by the staff of *De Telegraaf*, a daily newspaper that was heavily damaged in the riots and was hostile to the Provo movement.

Frenkel, F. E. *See* Regtien.

Fuchs, Johannes Marius. *Amsterdam, een lastige stad: Rellen, oproeren en opstanden in de loop der eeuwen*. Baarn: De Boekerij, 1970.

G. D. "Amerikanen en builenpest." *Gandalf* (Amsterdam) #21 (unpaged) (1967?). An interview with Huib Bronkhorst, father of the Provo Peter Bronkhorst.

Gadourek, Ivan. *A Dutch Community: Social and Cultural Structures and Process in a Bulb-Growing Region in the Netherlands*. Leiden: H. E. Stenfert-Kroese, 1956. A classic study of the effects of social segregation fostered by the Zuilen system, as seen in a typical Dutch town; text in English.

Galen, John Jansen Van (ed.). *Rumoer '66: een serie overdrukken uit de Haagse Post*. Amsterdam: Haagse Post, 1976. Articles on the late 1960s, reprinted from the news magazine *De Haagse Post* on the tenth anniversary of the June 14th riots. Includes articles on the Provos in general and on Van Duyn and Grootveld specifically.

Gasteren, Louis Van. *Allemaal rebellen: Amsterdam 1955–1965, een filmserie*. Amsterdam: Uitgeversmaatschappij Tabula, 1984.

Ginneken, Jaap Van. *Over de samenstelling van het gezamenlijk "Provo" Archief van het Seminarium voor Massapsychologie, Openbare Mening en Propaganda en de Universiteits-Bibliotheek*. Amsterdam: Universiteits-Bibliotheek, [1968?]. Catalog of the Provo Archives in the Handschriftkamer (Rare Book Room) of the Amsterdam University Library.

______. "Relletjes." Doctoral skriptie en werkstuk, Universiteit van Amsterdam. Amsterdam, 1970.

Grey Fox. "The Dutch Kabouters." *Roots*, No. 2 (New York: Ecology Action East, 1974), pp. 3–13. An interview with Roel Van Duyn in English.

______. "The Kabouters Demystified." *Roots*, No. 3 (New York: Ecology Action East, 1974), pp. 29–47. Includes interviews with Van Duyn and other Kabouters.

Grootveld, Robert Jasper. *See* Galen; Hendriks; Meier; Nedelandse Omroep Stichting; *Ratio*; Reeuwijk.

Haags Gemeentemuseum. (The Hague.) *New Babylon (een projekt van Constant Nieuwenhuys)*. Den Haag: Haags Gemeentemuseum, 1974. Illustrated.

Haftmann, Werner. *Painting in the Twentieth Century*. (2 Vols.) London: Humphries, 1960.

Hall, Gijsbert Van. *Ervaringen van een Amsterdammer (Memoirs of an Amsterdamer)*. Amsterdam: Elsevier, 1976. The autobiography of the man who was mayor of Amsterdam during the Provo period.

"Happenings Perpetuum Mobile." *Elseviers Weekblad*, July 16, 1966.

Hemmerijckx, Rik. "Ha, ha, happening: De Provo's in Brussel." *Amsab Tijdingen* (Gent: Archief en Museum van de Socialistische Abeidersbeweging) 19 (1993), pp. 12–15.

Hendriks, Nelleke. "Het speelse van Provo: De relatie met New Babylon en Robert Jasper Grootveld." Kandidaatscriptie Kunstgeschiedenis Universiteit van Amsterdam: Amsterdam, 1980.

Hofland, H. J. A. *Tegels lichten, of ware verhalen over de autoriteiten in het land van de voldongen feiten*. Amsterdam: Contact, 1972.

Houten, Hans ten. *De Provo's zijn fietsen- elk in eigen richting: Tien jaar geleden zetten ze zich in voor hun idealen- en nu?* Algemeen Dagblad. Juli 7, 1976, pp. 3–4.

Huges, Bart. *Transatlantic Review* no. 23 (Winter 1966/1967). An interview.

Hulsman, L. H. C. *Provo en de handhaving van de openbare orde*. De Gids v. 129:6–10 (1966) pp. 215–226.

Hummelink, Marcellinus B. E. "Après nous la liberté: Constant en de artistieke avant-garde in de jaren 1946–1960." Proefschrift Universiteit van Amsterdam. Amsterdam, 2002.

Jacobs, Leo. *Kleine Kaboutergids*. (AO-Reeks Boekje, 1319) Small-format brochure on the Kabouter movement.

Jacobs, Leonardo. "Provo: Verspreide opmerkingen over karakter en grondslagen van een lang durend kunstwerk." Doctoralscriptie Vakgroep Communicatiewetenschap, Universiteit van Amsterdam. Amsterdam, 1992.

Jaring, Cor. *Jaring's jaren '60: Beelden van een roerige tijd*. Cor Jaring, foto's; Simon Vinkenoog, teksten. Baarn: Kern, 1986. Primarily photographs.

______. *Je bent die je bent (en dat ben je)*. [*You Are Who You Are (and That's Who You Are)*.] Huizen [Netherlands]: Triton Pers, 1968. A first hand account of police brutality in Amsterdam by a noted photographer, pp. 44–48.

Jaring, Cor. *See also* Meier; Duijn, Roel Van.

Jorion, Paul. Quelques considerations relatives au phenomene "Provo." Bruxelles, [1968?]. Unpublished stenciled study of the movement, with much information and many Dutch texts translated into French.

Kabouterkrant. Amsterdam, 1970, Nos. 1–12. The official publication of the Kabouter movement.

Kaprow, Allan. See http://www.geocities.com/Athens/Acropolis/5422/kaprow.html

Kennedy, James C. *Nieuw Babylon in aanbouw: Nederland in de jaren zestig*. Amsterdam: Boom, 1997.

(Khayati, Mustapha) Situationist International. *On the poverty of student life considered in its economic, political, psychological, sexual, and particularly intellectual aspects, and a modest proposal for its remedy*. Originally printed in an edition of 10,000 by the Association fédérative générale des étudiants de Strausbourg in 1966, and republished in Chinese, French, and English by Éditions Champ Libre in 1972.

Kirby, Michael. *Happenings: An Illustrated Anthology*. New York: Dutton, 1966, c. 1965. A comprehensive account of the Happening.

Kleijer, Henk. "Spraakverwarring in Nieuw Babylon." *Sociologische Gids*, Nos. 5–6 (1997), pp. 421–432. Themanummer: Bouwen an Babylon:De jaren zestig in discussie.

Kleijn, Antonie. *Spelers buiten spel: Provocatie van gezag en maatschappij*. Alphen aan den Rijn: Samson, 1967.

Knip, Peter. *De Haagse Post over Provo*. Concept; Tijdschrift voor Maatschappijgeschiedenis 1:2 (Sept. 1984), pp. 89–104.

Kroes, Rob. *New Left, Nieuw Links, New Left: Verzet, beweging, verandering in Amerika, Nederland, Engeland*. Alphen aan den Rijn: Samson, 1975.

Kroes, Rob. *See also* Lastig Amsterdam.

Kultermann, Udo. *Art and Life*. New York: Praeger, 1971. An essay on the spirit of the Happening. Translation of Leben und Kunst.

Lambrecht, Jef. "Anarchisme bij Provo (Amsterdam 1965–1967)." Leuven: Department Sociologie, Fakulteit der Sociale Wetenschappen, Katholieke Universiteit te Leuven, 1974. A doctoral dissertation from the University of Louvain; text in Dutch. Not seen.

Lambrecht. *See* Nederlandse Omroep Stichting.

Lammers, Hans. "Vertrek van een burgemeester." *De Gids* (1967), pp. 369–374. (A prominent member of the Dutch Socialist Party disagrees with the manner in which Van Hall was fired.)

Lans, Jos Van der. *De werkelijkheid buiten spel: Over jeugdkultuur, Provo en jongerenbeweging*. Nijmegen:Katholieke Universiteit, 1981.

Lastig Amsterdam [*Bothersome Amsterdam*], edited by Rob Kroes. (Uitgave van de Nederlandse Sociologisch Vereeniging, #25) Den Haag, 1968.

Laufer, Robert S. *Institutionalization of Radical Movements and the Maintenance of Radical Identity in the Life Cycle*. [Paper] presented at the American Sociological Association Meetings, San Francisco, August 1975. Comparison of the Dutch and American New Left movements with reference to Provo.

Licht, Henri J. "The Dutch Provos: An Experiment in Political Activism." Melbourne [Australia], 1971. An unpublished stenciled seminar paper.

Lijphart, Arend. *The Politics of Accommodation: Pluralism and Democracy in the Netherlands*. (2nd revised edition.) Berkeley: University of California Press, 1975. A classic study of the Zuilen or social pillars that were a major societal determinant in Dutch society.

Luiters, Guus, [et al.]. *Hoera voor het prinselijk paar: een keuze uit Propria*

Cures, 1965–1973. Amsterdam: Arbeiderspers, 1975. Articles from the student newspaper on reactions to the royal wedding.

Mairowitz, David Zane. *See* Stansill.

Mamadouh, Virginie. *De stad in eigen hand: Provos, kabouters en Krakers als stedelijk sociale beweging.* [*Popular Control of City Government: Provos, Kabouters and Squatters as Urban Social Movement.*] Amsterdam: Sua, 1992.

Meier, Henk J. *Dit hap-hap happens in Amsterdam: een boodschap uit het Magisch Centrum Amsterdam in de vorm van foto's van Cor Jaring, tekst van Henk J. Meier en lay-out van Jacques Teljeur.* Amsterdam: De Arbeiderspers, 1966. A colorful account of the Happenings in Amsterdam and their relationship to the new Provo movement, this is the major source of information on Robert Jasper Grootveld; many photographs.

Mijn, Aad Van der. "Provo na de dood van Provo." *De Gids* (1967), pp. 134–136. An interview with Rob Stolk conducted in the final days of the Provo movement.

Motherwell, Robert. *The Dada Painters and Poets: An Anthology.* New York: Wittenborn, Schultz, 1951.

Mulisch, Harry. *Bericht aan de rattenkoning.* [*Report to the King of the Rats.*] Amsterdam: De Bezige Bij, 1967. A colorful account of the Provo movement by a leading Dutch novelist and commentator on social events.

Musée Picasso Antibes. *Constant: une rétrospective.* Antibes, Paris: Musée Picasso Antibes, Réunion des Musées Nationaux, 2001. Much information on the artist, including a biographical sketch.

Nabrink, Gé. *Drie baanbrekers: Leven en opvattingen van Ferdinand Domela Nieuwenhuis, J. Rutgers, Leo Polak.* Oosterwolde: Nordelijk Gewest van Vrije Socialisten, 1981. Includes a biographical sketch of Domela Nieuwenhuis.

Nederlandse Omroep Stichting. "Denkbeeld (Uitzending 29 november 1979) Onderwerp: De andere Nicolaas." Script of a radio program undertaken with the participation of Robert Jasper Grootveld and Jef Lambrecht, among others, on Sint Nicolaas, the Dutch Santa Claus.

Nieuwenhuys, Constant. "New Babylon." *Randstad*, No. 2, pp. 127–138. Amsterdam: De Bezige Bij, [1965?]. Text in Dutch.

______. "Opkomst van de avant-garde." *Randstad*, No. 8. Amsterdam: De Bezige Bij, [1968?].

______. *Opstand van de Homo Ludens.* [*Revolt of Joyous Humanity.*] Bussum: P. Brand, 1969. Constant's major statement of his beliefs.

______. *Von Cobra bis New Babylon.* Munchen [Munich]: Galerie Heseler, 1967. Catalog of an exhibition, including a text by Constant in German translation.

Nuis, Aad. *Wat is er gebeurd in Amsterdam?* [*What Has Happened in Am-*

sterdam?] Amsterdam: De Bezige Bij, 1966.

Otten, Marko. "Het pacifisme bij Provo." Groningen, 1982. Doctoralscreptie Rijksuniversiteit Groningen.

Pas, Niek. *Imaazje!: De verbeelding van Provo, 1965–1967.* [*Image!: The Imaging of Provo.*] Amsterdam: Wereldbibliotheek, 2003. Based on the author's doctoral dissertation, which is a major study that is overly skeptical and totally dismissive of the Provo movement; See my comments in Appendix 8.

Phaff, Johan. "Constant: 'De groeiende chaos is belangrijk, deze maatschappij heft geen schijn van kans meer': New Babylon, maar eerst de revolutie." *Rij Nederland*, September 3, 1970, pp. 9–10.

Plomp, Hans. *See* Bogers.

Poppel, C. B. P. Van. "De Amsterdam Provos uit de jaren 1965–1967." Amsterdam, 1968. Unpublished manuscript.

POR, No. 3 [1967?]. Leeuwarden. A Provo magazine from Friesland province.

Poster, Mark. *Existential Marxism in Postwar France from Sartre to Althusser*. Princeton: Princeton University Press, 1977, c.1975.

Propria Cures Jaargang 77, No. 29 (May 27, 1967), "Special Issue for English-Speaking Visitors to the Magic Centre of the World." An English language issue of the student newspaper of the University of Amsterdam that contains a tongue-in-cheek guide to riots in Amsterdam: where to find them and where to find legal and medical aid.

Provo. Amsterdam: Provo, 1965–1967, Numbers 1–15. The magazine of the Provo movement.

Raam (Amsterdam), Vol. 4 (January 1968), pp. 6–12.

Racine, Aimée. *See* Vassart.

Radcliffe, Charles. *See Anarchy*; and Rosemont.

Ratio: Literair Maandblad, (Amsterdam) #13 (January–February 1965) "Dit nummer is een happening." ["This Issue is a Happening."] A special issue of *Ratio, a Literary Monthly*, on the Happenings, including "Een warning" ["A Warning"], by Grootveld and texts by Vinkenoog and Posthuma.

Reeuwijk, Dick P. J. Van. *Damsterdamse extremisten, met een bijdrage van Cees Noordewier*. [*Amsterdam Extremists.*] Amsterdam: De Bezige Bij, 1965. Includes chapters which give important information on Grootveld, Bart Huges, the Happenings, and the Provos.

Regtien, Ton, and Konrad Boehmer. *Van Provo tot Oranje Vrijstaat*. [*From Provo to Orange Freestate.*] Amsterdam: Socialistische Uitgeverij, 1970. A communist critique primarily concerned with the Kabouter movement.

Regtien, Ton. In Frenkel, F. E. (editor), *Provo: kentekeningen bij een deelverschijnsel*. Amsterdam: Polak & Van Gennep, 1967.

Richter, Hans. *Dada, Art and Anti-Art*. New York: Thames & Hudson, 1965.

Righart, Hans. *De eindeloze jaren zestig: Geschiedenis van een generatieconflict*. Amsterdam: Arbeiderspers, 1995.

Rooij, Maarten. "A Constitutional Question: The Marriage of Princess Beatrix." *Delta* (Amsterdam), Vol. 9, Nos. 1–2 (Spring/Summer 1966). An informative article on constitutional issues involved in the marriage of the princess.

Rosemont, Franklin, and Charles Radcliffe. *Dancin' in the Streets: Anarchists, IWWs, Surrealists, Situationists & Provos in the 1960s as recorded in the pages of The Rebel Worker & Heatwave*. Chicago: Charles H. Kerr, 2005. Contains Charles Radcliffe's eyewitness accounts of the developing Provo situation. Particularly fascinating for Radcliffe's analysis of Provo's theoretical positioning.

Sartre, Jean-Paul. *Between Existentialism and Marxism*. New York: Pantheon, 1974.

______. *Critique of Dialectical Reason. I. Theory of Practical Ensembles*. London: Verso/New Left Books; New York: Schocken, 1976. Translation of *Critique de la raison dialectique*, originally published by Gallimard, Paris, 1960. A major but largely neglected analysis of history and revolutionary activity, which predicted the fate of the Provo movement and the May 1968 revolt in France, seven and eight years before their occurrence.

Scheepmaker, Nico. "Amsterdams kwartier." *Holland Maandblad* (April 1967), pp. 15–18. An amusing eyewitness account of the Prinsengracht riot.

Schenk, M. G. *Prins Claus*. Baarn: De Boekerij, 1972.

Het slechste uit Provo. *See* Duyn, Roel Van.

Schierbeek, Bert. *The Experimental Artists*. Amsterdam: Meulenhoff, [196-?]. A short lively essay on the Cobra artists by a Vijftiger poet.

Schippers, K. *Holland Dada*. Amsterdam: Querido, 1974.

Schoolenberg, Hans, and Jasper Van der Zee. "De Provobeweging." ["The Provo Movement."] Werkstuk in het kader van de S. O. Groep, "Waarom D'66, PPr en DS 70?" Amsterdam, 1975. Typewritten manuscript on liberal splinter groups from the conservative political parties and on the Provo influence in this development.

Schoondergang, Huub. *...Een toen kwamen de Kabouters: Van jeugdbeweging tot bewogen jeugd*. [*...Then Came the Kabouters: From Youth Movement to Troubling Youth*.] Leiden: A. W. Sijthoff, 1971. On post-war youth in the Netherlands.

Shetter, William Z. *The Pillars of Society: Six Centuries of Civilization in the*

Netherlands. The Hague: Nijhoff, 1971. Chapters 2 and 14 give an interesting summary of the impact of the Sixties on the traditional values in Dutch society.

Siepel, Alwin. "Moedwil en misverstand: Provo en de beeldvorming in de pers 1965–1967." *Aanzet* 12:2 (1994), pp. 129–146.

Singer, Daniel. *Prelude to Revolution: The May Revolt in France*. New York: Hill & Wang, 1970. A comprehensive account of the May 1968 revolt in France, which had many parallels with the Provo movement.

Sinner, Louis. *Provos en justitie*. [*Provos and Justice*.] Amsterdam: De bezige Bij, 1966.

Snelders, Stephen. *See* Bogers.

Stack, George J. "Sartre's Dialectic of Social Relations." Philosophy and Phenomenological Research (Buffalo), Vol. 31 (March 1971), pp. 394–408.

Stansill, Peter, and David Zane Mairowitz. *BAMN (By Any Means Necessary): Outlaw Manifestos and Ephemera, 1965–70*. Harmondsworth: Penguin, 1971. Republished by Autonomedia in 1998. An excellent anthology of leftist activist manifestos from Western Europe and the United States with an appendix of texts in the original languages. For the Netherlands see chapters 1, 3, 11, and 12.

Stokvis, Willemijn. *Cobra: geschiedenis, voorspel en betekenis van een beweging in de kunst van na de Tweede Wereldoorlog*. [*Cobra: History, Introduction and Significance of Post-World War II Art Movement*.] Amsterdam: De Bezige Bij, 1974. Monograph on the Cobra movement. Much information on Constant Nieuwenhuys.

Tasman, Coen. "Immazje! Imaazje!: De ontwikkeling van Provo van locale "rebellenclub" tot een international symbol van de roerige jaren zestig." Buiten de Orde (Herfst, 2003). A critical review of Niek Pas' book, *Imaazje! De verbeelding van Provo, 1965–1967*.

______. *Louter Kabouter: Kroniek van een beweging, 1969–1974*. [*Pure Kabouter: Chronicle of a Movement*.] Amsterdam: Babylon-De Geus, 1996. The major work on the Kabouter Movement by a member of that group.

Tegenbosch, Lambert. "Een avondje in December." ["An Evening in December."] *Raam*, No. 41 (januari 1968), pp. 6–12. About Grootveld in Maastricht.

Thoenes, Piet. "Rebels from Affluence: The Provos of Holland." *The Nation*, Vol. 204 (April 17, 1967), pp. 494–497.

Tijen, Tjebbe Van. *Je bevrijden van de drukpers: Jongeren en hun eigen pers in Nederland, 1945–1990*. Amsterdam: Internationaale Instituut voor Sociale Geschiedenis, 1993.

Tijn, J. Van. "De krenten zijn nu wel uitgedeeld: Provo in een nieuwe fase." ["The Raisins Have Been Parceled Out: Provo in a New Phase."] *Vrij Nederland*, March 4, 1967, p. 7.

Troeltsch, Ernst. *The Social Teachings of the Christian Church.* (2 Vols.) London: Allen & Unwin; New York: Macmillan, 1931. Many subsequent editions.

Tuynman, Hans. *Full-Time Provo.* Amsterdam: De Bezige Bij, 1967. The autobiographical account of a Provo whose imprisonment sparked major demonstrations. The text is in Dutch, the English title notwithstanding.

Van Provo tot Groenevelt: tien jaar verandering zoals geregistreerd in De Nieuwe Linie. Samenstelling, Joos Aarts, et al. Amsterdam: De Nieuwe Linie/Van Gennep, 1973. A selection of articles reprinted from De Nieuwe Linie, a leftist newspaper, including articles on Van Duyn, the Maagdehuis seizure, and a debate between Van Duyn and Ton Regtien.

Vassart, Christian et Aimée Racine. *Provos et provotariat: un an de recherche participante en milieu provo.* Bruxelles: CEDJ (Centre d'Etude de la Delinquence Juvenile), 1968. (CEDJ Publication No. 21.) A study of the Provo groups in Belgium and the Netherlands.

Verhellen, E. *De provobeweging: Bijdrage tot een juistere begripomschrijving.* Gent: Rijksuniversiteit Gent, 1978.

Verkerk, Corrie. "Uche- een rookmagier blikt terug." *Het Parool,* 18 juli 1992. An interview with Robert Jasper Grootveld.

Viénet, René. *Enragés and Situationists in the Occupation Movement, France, May '68.* New York: Autonomedia, 1992.

Vinkenoog, Simon. *See Ratio*; Jaring.

Voeten, Teun. "Dutch Provos." *High Times* (January 1990), pp. 32–36, 64–66, 73. Interesting review, in English, of the Provos.

Vossen, Koen. "Roel van Duijn over Provo's, Kabouters en jongeren van nu." *Aanzet* 12:2 (1994), pp. 101–115.

Vrij Nederland (Amsterdam) June 13, 1970, p. 5.

Weerlee, Duco Van. *Wat de Provos willen.* [*What the Provos Want.*] Amsterdam: De Bezige Bij, 1966.

"White Bicycle Plan, The." *Delta* (Amsterdam), Vol. 10, No. 3 (Autumn 1967), pp. 39–40.

Wigley, Mark. *Constant's New Babylon: The Hyper-Architecture of Desire.* Rotterdam: Witte de With/Center for Contemporary Architecture, 010 Publishers, 1998.

More Books from Autonomedia